MUSEUM OF ART SÃO PAULO

MUSEUM OF ART SÃO PAULO

Newsweek / GREAT MUSEUMS OF THE WORLD

NEW YORK, N.Y.

**GREAT MUSEUMS
OF THE WORLD**

American Editor:
Henry A. La Farge

MUSEUM OFART SÃO PAULO

Introduction by:
Pietro Maria Bardi

Text by:
Curatorial Staff of the
São Paulo Museum

Photographs:
Romulo Fialdini

Design:
Aldo Tonella
Armando Garcia

Published by
NEWSWEEK, INC.
& ARNOLDO MONDADORI EDITORE

ISBN 0-88225-246-1
Library of Congress Card No. 81-47855
© 1978 — Companhia Melhoramentos de São Paulo
Indústrias de Papel
Rua Tito, 479 — São Paolo

English text © 1981 — Arnoldo Mondadori Editore S.p.A., Milano

INTRODUCTION

PIETRO MARIA BARDI
Director

The São Paulo Museum of Art, which owes its existence to the founder, Assis Chateaubriand, is somewhat different from other museums. It is also one of the youngest, having been inaugurated on October 2, 1947. It was thus obliged to make up for lost time in order to organize a significant collection. Taking advantage of Brazil's post-World War II economic growth, we had unusual opportunities for acquiring works of art from the numerous European collections which had entered the market as a result of the war. This volume presents only a part of the Museum's collection, chosen to give the reader an idea of their varied nature and the criteria used in the selection, besides offering a panorama of all the artistic schools and periods represented.

The founding of the Museum was an ambitious project—perhaps too ambitious, full of difficulties and sometimes almost impossibilities. However, we were convinced that as Brazil advanced in industrial prosperity, it would gradually intensify its cultural activities and permit us to collect the type of works which would fulfill our museological aspirations. The aim of our Museum was never simply to collect works of art, but also to create a center for the spread of cultural concerns. We intended to foster educational activities so that our visitors would be able to appreciate the meaning of original works of art.

The organization of this unique Museum and its establishment within a cultural atmosphere still dependent upon the romantic "art for art's sake" doctrine and controlled by the demands of "academicism" involved exciting and challenging experiences. We started from scratch and worked continuously and simultaneously in the most disparate fields. In the artistic microsociety of São Paulo, we had to confront two conflicting types: the jealous conservative with his old-fashioned, academic beliefs; and the innovator, with a futuristic background and visionary ideas. The first believed that the city already had its museum, the State one; the second unfurled Marinetti's complaints about museums and called for their destruction—why a museum in a city like São Paulo with its demographic explosion?

It was Chateaubriand's idea to establish a museum. We created it together with the cordial friendship of kindred spirits. Many people saw a parallel in our situation with that of Chicago. However, that somewhat similar city always had an aesthetic substratum which, although tied to economic factors, possessed unique characteristics that held decisive promise for the development of the arts. It is sufficient to point to the Chicago School, with its masters from Sullivan to Wright.

São Paulo in 1947 was a city in search of an urban order, an eclectic scheme of architecture, but there was little artistic production. The "Week of Modern Art" in 1922 had been an attempt to break out of this aesthetic inertia, but it supplied no positive proposals. It was followed by a short period of excitement and later one of apathy, in spite of the activities of some poets, such as Mário de Andrade and Oswald de Andrade.

Accordingly, the Museum had to be inaugurated taking into account the recent past and the present needs. We acted judiciously to avoid a clash with those faithful to the *status quo* and those who were unprepared to confront or comprehend contemporary aesthetic questions, which was the more time-consuming task. Because we were unable to surmount the conservatives' concept of a traditional museum, we decided upon a completely innovative plan. The 1,000 square-meter space placed at our disposal in Chateaubriand's new Diários Associados Building was utilized with the idea of a cultural activities center rather than as a museum *per se.* The area was divided in the following manner: (1) hall for permanent acquisitions; (2) space for didactic exhibitions of art history; (3) auditorium; (4) temporary exhibition hall. We soon presented our first acquisitions, all original works of art. We provided informative surveys with good illustrations, easily read commentaries and legends (at that time, art books in Portuguese were still rather rare); we organized lecture dedicated to art history and aesthetics; we held exhibitions of the few widely discussed Brazilian artists, and later foreign artists.

The Museum became, in this way, a meeting place for those initiated in art and for those in pursuit of knowledge. It was planned to be responsive to different types of demands, although not all pertinent to its function, such as an agricultural exhibition, a beauty contest, etc. No limits were placed on artistic activites. Naturally, there were chamber concerts, and, when more space became available, an auditorium for drama, films and musical shows was constructed. Even operas were presented; Stravinsky's *Histoire d'un soldat,* for example, had its Brazilian debut in our small theatre.

Three years after its founding, the Museum had a considerably larger space and vastly expanded its activities. Courses in industrial design, advertising, gardening, and dance, as well as a seminar on films were opened. The classes were staffed by the most respected teachers, each one conscious of the problems involved in the dissemination of culture, including the painters Lasar Segall and Roberto Sambonet, the sculptor August Zamoyski, the architects Lina Bo Bardi and Gian Carlos Palanti, and the film-maker Alberto Cavalcanti.

A young peoples' orchestra was started; just a few years later, it was considered one of the best in Brazil. A professional and a children's ballet corps were organized. One thousand school children visited the Museum daily. We were obliged to occupy two more floors—the Museum space then totaled 4,000 square meters.

The temporary exhibitions became more and more important and a true attraction for the public, which increased monthly. The exhibition dedicated to Le Corbusier was a great success. It included Le Corbusier's original plans for the Ministry of Education and Health offices in Rio de Janeiro, his 1936 plans for the urban development of the capital, and his paintings and sculptures. The exhibition travelled to several European capitals.

Other important exhibitions were dedicated to: Max Bill, which resulted in the beginning of the concretist movement in Brazil; Saul Steinberg, which included a group of unpublished drawings; Alexander Calder, with mobiles, jewelry, and the prestigious presence of the artist; the School of Paris; contemporary Italian design; German Expressionist graphics; the complete engravings of Käthe Kollwitz; and so on. From these, the reader can gain a general idea of the level of the exhibitions. We presented shows based on historical themes, such as: French portraiture from Fouquet to Prud'hon, with works loaned by Georges Wildenstein of Paris; the poster, with originals by Toulouse-Lautrec and Chéret; the architecture of country homes by Richard Neutra; illustrations from editions of *Don Quixote*. All these and many similar initiatives reveal that our institution has continually been more dedicated to the dissemination of art history and encouragement of contemporary artistic activity than simply to conservation. Our organization was and continues to be an authentic laboratory for the elaboration and discussion of artistic values with the aim of opening paths for the comprehension of living art.

While all these activities flourished, the Museum's collection continued to grow. Because this is the topic that most concerns the reader, we will talk more about that particular adventure. Lionello Venturi, in an essay dedicated to the Museum, described our activities in a rather picturesque manner: he likened them to a pilgrim going from Italy to Mecca—which is not in Arabia but in Brazil. Simultaneously with the founding of the Museum in 1947, we began to purchase works. Assis Chateaubriand was the owner and director of a large chain of newspapers, magazines, radio stations and, in that very year, he became the pioneer of television in Latin America. He was also involved in awakening the Brazilian consciousness to aviation, organizing fleets of training aircraft to be donated to recently-created airplane clubs; he himself donated almost one thousand planes. Satisfied with the results of this project, he devoted his energies to organizing public contributions for a museum which would initially function in Rio de Janeiro, but would later be transferred to São Paulo, in consideration of the economic power of the coffee industry and the substantial industrial activities growing up around it.

It was Chateaubriand's intention to give the Museum a true national character, and contributions were solicited from every part of Brazil, from Pôrto Vehlo in the Rondônia Territory to Pôrto Alegre in Rio Grande do Sul State. He used the same technique that had been successful in the creation of the airplane clubs. However, while everyone easily understood the importance of linking and integrating the nation with air service, it was a more difficult task to explain the acquisition of works of art. Planes cost a set price, but people felt that paintings were astronomically high. Chateaubriand was well acquainted with the psychology of his wealthy compatriots and invented a unique system to provide resources for the Museum. He asked for contributions to educate our young people and simultaneously offered these maecenas promotional support in the press. Many legends circulate about Chateaubriand's activities, but the truth is that this "builder of the future" acted with justice and tenacity in all areas. His intelligence and imagination led him to unusual ways of gaining attention. Before a work entered the Museum's collection, it was always exhibited and fêted in one of the elegant mansions of Rio or São Paulo or another state capital. It received attention on radio, television, and on the front pages of the *Diários Associados* newspapers. The mention of the maecenas' names resulted in a large increase in philanthropists. This example of public spirit had already occurred in the United States of America.

To have Titian, Renoir, or Matisse received with applause, panegyrics and champagne aroused the interest of the well-to-do names in agriculture, commerce, and industry. Some of these celebrations occurred in the Museum itself; others in public plazas, such as the presentation of van Gogh's *Schoolboy* in an unprecedented public festival in Campo Grande, Salvador, Bahia, in which all the schools participated. These receptions became an institution and public interest grew and grew. Thus, it was possible to consolidate a group of "Friends of the Museum," who were willing to go along with requests for new purchases.

The history of the donations to the Museum is rich in picturesque happenings which Chateaubriand has spiritedly narrated. On one occasion, during a reception for Chester Dale at the National Gallery in Washington, Chateaubriand asked in a loud voice that Americans drink more of our coffee in order for Brazil's economy to prosper and for the Museum to be able to

12

further enrich its collections. Mixing coffee export with cultural manipulation, Chateaubriand planned his safaris into the jungle of the wealthy with a shotgun made of parties. At times, to persuade philanthropists to participate in the development of the Museum, he provoked caustic polemics. Chateaubriand even created the "Order of the Backlandsmen," and initiated that spirited Sir Winston Churchill in a special ceremony, after Churchill had promised to give the Museum one of his paintings.

How, when, and where did we make our purchases? Our techniques for acquisitions were based on the decision to deal with the most respected European and North American galleries. We chose Knoedler, Matthiesen, Marlborough, Seligmann and Daber, as well as several dealer-collectors. But it was with Wildenstein in particular that Chateaubriand established a most enduring friendship, and the late Georges Wildenstein became dedicated to the Museum. In 1953, owing to the unlimited credit supplied to us and Mr. Wildenstein's sound technical advice as an extraordinary connoisseur, it was possible for us to substantially develop our holdings. These attained such a volume that in that same year we received several invitations to present an exhibition at several European museums.

The proposed tour also helped to answer some of the vicious commentaries which some sectors of the press directed at the Museum and at the quality of its collection. The cultural atmosphere was not yet ready to critically evaluate the works we purchased. For outsiders it seemed impossible for Brazil to possess masterpieces of such importance. Indeed, when it was announced that one hundred paintings from São Paulo would be exhibited in the *Orangerie* at the Louvre at the request of the French Government, one Rio de Janeiro newspaper immediately carped that they would return rather quickly because the French experts would judge many of them to be fakes. No other museum could have endured the misfortunes and problems which tormented the establishment of our Museum. But early on we had anticipated that these difficulties would occur. There were even diplomatic stumbling blocks. When our exhibition was to open at the *Orangerie,* it was impossible to convince our Embassy to invite the President of the French Republic to its inauguration. However, through personal contacts, President Auriol presided at the opening. The exhibition proved a huge critical success and the public attendance was exceptional.

The fame of the Museum abroad was largely due to this exhibition. We were invited to present it at the Palais des Beaux-Arts in Brussels, at the Centraal Museum in Utrecht, the Kunstmu-   13 seum in Berne, the Tate Gallery in London, the Kunsthalle of Düsseldorf and the Palazzo Reale of Milan. Afterwards, we rejected other European invitations in order to accept that of the Metropolitan Museum of New York. Other North American museums extended invitations, but we only exhibited at the Museum of Fine Arts in Toledo, Ohio. The tour wound up with an exhibition at Rio de Janeiro's Museu Nacional de Belas Artes.

At that time, the Museum entered into loan agreements with a North American bank in order to acquire another group of works. Many economic commentators questioned our acquisitions plan. It was a simple one, which relied on two facts: a belief in the probable rise in market values in the years following the war; and the possibility of buying on credit. Our calculations, based on detailed investigations of the market, convinced us that the value of the Impressionists, for example, would go up between 20% and 25% after 1950. Based on this conviction and on our being able to obtain money at 4% interest, we believed that our plans would be successful. In addition, we entered the market with the reputation for making quick decisions about purchases, while other museums had to await the approval of their Board of Trustees. Once again, we were successful by not following the economists. A large part of our collection was purchased through options by telegram, followed up by immediate verifications; owing to our continuous travel, we were nicknamed "globe-trotters." It was an unusual experience, but quite typical of a moving force such as Chateaubriand.

I am well aware that our collection could have been more homogenous. Its organization was influenced by several uncontrollable circumstances such as: the requirement to purchase paintings in lots; the philanthropist's taste, which imposed, for example, a preference for Renoir over other painters; the rejection of artists with vanguard tendencies; and donations which could not be refused. The composition of a collection, when not under one sole director, must, by force, tolerate interferences which are not always constructive. Although we know that history is not written with "if," it is worthwhile to stress that if instead of possessing thirteen Renoirs we had only six and in place of the other seven we had works by Géricault, Bonington, Sisley, Jongkind, Theodore Rousseau, Daubigny, Millet and others, we would be no less admirers of that Impressionist master. The same can be said of Modigliani: of the six portraits in the Museum, the director would be glad to keep a minimum of three, and exchange the others for canvases by Braque, Bacon, Van Dongen, etc. Thus, we have in mind future exchanges to balance our Museum's collection.

We made the decision to present works in a system of rotation as a result of a study carried out among our visitors. A fixed collection has little chance of being enriched. It is of interest to the visitor on only one occasion. However, when the visitor knows that new works are constantly being placed on view, his return to the museum becomes a habit. With this in mind, we periodically change our Museum's composition and include, at times, individual or collective shows of high quality.

This "anti-museum" system has given us good results with our viewing public, which is still somewhat inexperienced in the field of art, although gradually participating more and more in our "laboratory." Our undertaking could not have been possible without the clear and full support of government agencies, like our Ministries of the Treasury, Education, and Culture, as well as our Ministry of Foreign Affairs, and naturally, the leaders of our nation.

Our new building, planned by the architect Lina Bo Bardi, was inaugurated in 1968 by Queen Elizabeth II of England. It was constructed for us by the City Council of São Paulo. As you will see at the end of this volume in the pages devoted to the building itself, the physical structure corresponds to needs which have existed since the Museum first came into being in 1947: an atmosphere which serves as an activities center for contemporary artistic life, rather than merely a place for the conservation of works of art. In fact, when the Museum was founded, we presented it as a "museological cell," keeping in mind the modern concept of a museum and, at the same time, the future possibility of São Paulo's having a large collection and conserving it in a museum which was more active than the conventional type.

P. M. Bardi

ITALY

ADEODATO ORLANDI. *The Crucifixion.*

This panel is a document of twelfth-century Italian painting which synthe-
sizes the early tradition of Lucca with the intensely dramatic currents
which had their origin in the art of Cimabue. Adeodato Orlandi was to a
certain extent influenced by Cimabue. This is especially evident in the better
conserved parts of this panel, such as the four symbols of the Evangelists
and the figures of Saint Peter and Saint Paul. In this small space the painter
concentrated the moral and expressive grandeur of the mural compositions
of the period.

BERNARDO DADDI. *Madonna and Child.* *p. 19*

Bernardo Daddi was an important Florentine painter of the generation following Giotto and the Sienese painter, Duccio di Buoninsegna. Both of
these tendencies co-exist in his work: the proto-humanism of Giotto—who
initially influenced Daddi—and the Gothic tradition which was still alive in

ADEODATO ORLANDI
Lucca, active 1288-1308
*The Crucifixion, with Mary and
Saint John among Saints*
Tempera on panel; 45 x 47 cm.
In the Museum since 1947.

BERNARDO DADDI
Florence, c. 1290-Florence, c. 1348
Madonna and Child (c. 1340)
Tempera on panel, gold background;
66 x 39 cm.
Belonged to Julius Böhler,
Munich; then to the art historian
F.M. Perkins, Lastra a Signa.
In the Museum since 1958.

FRANCESCO BOTTICINI
Florence, c. 1446-Florence, c. 1497.
Madonna Adoring the Child Jesus
Tempera on panel; 74 x 54 cm.
In the Museum since 1947.

Facing page
PSEUDO PIER FRANCESCO FIORENTINO
Florence, active second half of the fifteenth century
Madonna with the Child Jesus, Saint John and an Angel
Tempera on wood, gold background;
diameter 105 cm.
Inscription on the frame,
engraved in the panel:
*LAUDAMUS TE GLORIA IN EXCELSIS
DEO ET IN TERRA PAX HOMINIBUS
BONE VOLUNTATIS.*
In the Museum since 1947.

MAESTRO DEL BAMBINO VISPO
Florence, active first decades
of the fifteenth century
Adoration of the Magi
Tempera on panel; 35 x 32 cm.
In the Museum since 1947.

20

21

Siena. In this attractive panel, he presents a sweetly human Virgin who smiles at her little son with tenderness, and a surprisingly vivacious Child who plays with the collar of her cloak and one of her fingers. Although Giottesque in their expressions, the figures stand out from the gold background with the decorative rhythm and the chromatic sensibilities of the Sienese masters, whose influence appears to have prevailed during the painter's maturity.

FRANCESCO BOTTICINI. *Madonna Adoring the Child Jesus.* p. 20

The absorbed attitude of the Virgin and the angel, and the realism of the Child, against the excessive rigidity of the architectural setting led this work and others by Botticini to be confused with and attributed in the nineteenth century to Botticelli and Ghirlandaio. Nevertheless, the ample and sinuous design, the density of the colors, and the novelty of the landscape of Florence in the background confer a peculiar originality upon the panel which came to be recognized as the mark of Botticini.

PSEUDO PIER FRANCESCO FIORENTINO. *Madonna with the Child Jesus, Saint John and an Angel.* p. 21

This tondo which, with the exception of the delicately expressive face of the Virgin, is somewhat simple-minded and conventional, is attributed to a possible disciple of Filippo Lippi or of Pesellino—an artisan painter erroneously identified as Pier Francesco Fiorentino. He is a characteristic lesser Florentine master whose technique, in comparison with Pier Francesco, is still somewhat uncertain, but more refined.

MAESTRO DEL BAMBINO VISPO. *Adoration of the Magi.* p. 20

The critic Sirén at the beginning of the century attempted to reconstruct the personality of this unknown painter—distantly related to Lorenzo Monaco. He gave him the name of *Maestro del Bambino Vispo* (Master of the Vivacious Child) owing to his characteristic presentation of the Child smiling and playing in the Virgin's lap. Sirén included this panel of the Magi among the vast work left by the artist. In any case, we have here a typical depiction by a pre-Renaissance painter still influenced by the Gothicism of the Sienese masters but, nonetheless, permeated with a happy naturalness.

GIOVANNI BELLINI. *Madonna and Christ Child.* p. 23

One of the Museum's most famous paintings is Giovanni Bellini's so-called "Willys Madonna"—after the name of its penultimate owner. The son of Jacopo and brother of Gentile, and a central figure of Venetian painting during the fifteenth and early sixteenth centuries, Giovanni Bellini is seen here still following Mantegna's sculpturesque manner, yet already predicting the new directions of Giorgione's tonalism. The Master in this painting attains rich vibrations of chiaroscuro and soft luminosity, which seem to reflect the clarity of the atmosphere in the lateral landscapes.

GIOVANNI BELLINI
Venice, c. 1430-Venice 1516
Madonna and Christ Child (c. 1488)
oil on panel; 75 x 59 cm.
Signed on the parapet:
JOANNES BELLINUS.
From the collection of Sir George Campbell, Glasgow, it passed to Lord Duveen, London, and later to John N. Willys, Toledo, Ohio. In the Museum since 1957.

23

ANDREA MANTEGNA.   *Saint Jerome.*

The acceptance of this panel as an autograph work of the artist was confirmed by the invitation for it to be included in the great Mantegna exhibition which took place in Mantua in 1960. The sculpturesque organization and the typical fifteenth-century frontality of the figure confer on it an epic monumental tension. This passionate evocation of antiquity was transmitted to the young Mantegna by his teacher Squarcione in Padua, and heightened by his contacts with the Bellinis and the Tuscan painters active in the Veneto: Paolo Uccello, Filippo Lippi and Andrea del Castagno. In this panel, the creator of the *"Camera degli Sposi"* transfigures reality with stony, incorruptible forms, delineated in metallic contours.

PIERO DI COSIMO (PIERO DI LORENZO).   *Madonna with Christ Child and Saint John.*   *p. 26*

This tondo full of movement with its agreeable colors presents an adolescent Madonna carrying in one hand the small Christ Child, who already appears conscious of his future mission, and with the other hand caressing the plump Saint John. The rhythm of the composition against the pleasant green landscape and waters is established by the angel picking flowers and the delightful detail of the merle gluttonously looking at a large caterpillar.

24

ANDREA MANTEGNA
Isola di Carturo 1431-Mantua 1506
Saint Jerome (c. 1449–1450)
Oil on panel; 48 x 36 cm.
Belonged to Prince Paul
of Yugoslavia.
In the Museum since 1952.

FRANCIA (FRANCESCO RAIBOLINI). *Madonna with the Christ Child and Saint John.* *Facing page*

Francesco di Marco Raibolini—who declared himself "Il Francia" in homage to his first teacher, a Frenchman—represents the point of contact between the Ferrara style of Francesco Cossa and Lorenzo Costa on the one hand, and the style of the Umbrian School on the other, especially Perugino, whose influence is well known. In his work, the lustrous modelling of the surfaces is joined with color of extreme purity. In the opinion of the critic Roberto Longhi, this panel must have been executed in the last years of the painter's activity, at approximately the same time as the Buonvisi Retable, dated 1511 and now in the National Gallery, London. This appears to be confirmed by the striking analogy in the luminous, almost glasslike enamel paint surface of the two paintings, together with the brilliant colors harmonizing the figures and the landscape. The compositional invention is also notable; the figures of the Christ Child playing with Saint John's small cross are probably attributable to a workshop collaborator.

FRANCIA (FRANCESCO RAIBOLINI)
Bologna, c. 1450-Bologna 1517
Madonna with Christ Child and Saint John
Oil on panel; 63 x 48 cm.
From the collection of
Lord Crawford, Wigan, Liverpool.
In the Museum since 1947.

PIERO DI COSIMO
(PIERO DI LORENZO)
Florence 1462-Florence 1521
Madonna with Christ Child and Saint John
Oil on panel; diameter 129 cm.
During the nineteenth century, in the
Kunsthistorisches Museum, Vienna.
Then sold and entered the collection
of Baron W. Offenheim, Vienna, who deposited it
in the Rijksmuseum, Amsterdam,
where it was exhibited from 1933 to 1937.
During this time it was described
in several essays as being in Holland.
In the Museum since 1951.

RAPHAEL. *Resurrection of Christ.* *p. 29*

Some works of art have a history cloaked in mystery—itineraries, forgotten moments, exaltations, good or bad encounters, and speculative claims of all kinds. But the day finally arrives when enthusiasm and love put them in their merited place, often in a museum. That is the story of this panel. It was found in New York in the Easter season of 1954. An amateur-dealer had consigned it to a collector who offered it to us as a Raphael without any bibliographic background whatsoever, totally hiding its provenance. He asked a high price while stating at the same time that another museum had already decided to buy it at the moment we were tempted to say no. We had to decide then and there. After examining it, with intuition overshadowing knowledge, opinions and questions, the acquisition was made, with appropriate appeals to the goddess Fortune. It was then decided to send the "Raphael" for exhibition at the Tate Gallery. By word of mouth, in spite of the smiles of the competitors, we found out some information: Berenson had attributed *"Resurrection"*—which had appeared at Christie's in 1946—to Mariano de Ser Austerio, a very modest painter of altar frontals in the style of Perugino. The attribution by such an authority was peremptory, sufficient enough to veto any activity. To insert the discovery—which was no longer a discovery—at the Tate exhibition as a work of Raphael was judged a daring, or at least, an imprudent act. Philip James, Director of the British Council, our host, offered the following solution: it was agreed that the catalogue would place the responsibility for attribution with the director of the Brazilian Museum. Taking advantage of bibliographical sources available in London, we were able to establish the initial fact which broke the barrier of originality: Cavalcaselle, in his *Rafaello* of 1884, had noted some information received from Bode who had seen the panel in 1880 in the collection of Lord Kinnaird in Rossie Priory. J. van Regteren Altena, visiting Rossie Priory in 1927, discovered that two Raphael drawings kept in the Ashmolean Museum in Oxford were related to the two soldier figures in the painting under discussion. These elements helped us to conclude that the "Resurrection" was an autograph work of Perugino's young studio assistant. The situation became even more complicated when the painting was exhibited at the Royal Palace in Milan, Italy: there were insinuations in which the invective surpassed ignorance. It was doubted that the painting was the one from Rossie Priory. Finally, a long study by Roberto Longhi in *Paragone* in 1965, *"Percorso de Raffaello giovane,"* reestablished the complete truth. In the masterpiece, done during the years he was working in small format, Raphael appears to employ memories of Melozzo da Forli and Pintoricchio. The *Resurrection* is from that moment; the digressions on the techniques of Pintoricchio are evident. The controversies over, the attribution to Raphael was finally resolved and the *Resurrection* began to circulate under its paternity: Raphael.

28

RAPHAEL (RAFFAELLO SANTI)
Urbino 1483-Rome 1520
Resurrection of Christ (c. 1503)
Oil on panel; 52 x 44 cm.
From the collection of Lord Kinnaird,
Rossie Priory, Perthshire, England,
it passed to the collection of
Thomas Harris, London.
In the Museum since 1954.

TITIAN. *Cardinal Cristoforo Madruzzo.*

The monumental splendor of this great portrait offers an appropriate characterization of one of the most important participants in the Council of Trent. Cardinal Madruzzo's extraordinarily expressive face stands out against the triple chromatic contrast of the red of the velvet curtain, the dark green of the wall, and the black area of the immense robe sparsely broken by the edges of the collar and the cuffs, and his hand holding the breviary. This majestic harmony is attained through extremely simple means.

TITIAN (TIZIANO VECELLIO)
Pieve di Cadore, c. 1485-Venice 1576
Cardinal Cristoforo Madruzzo
Oil on canvas; 210 x 109 cm.
Signed and dated, with inscription
at top right:
ANNO DNI MDLII AETATIS
SUAE XXXVIIII TITIAN FECIT.
On the clock, the date: *1552.*
This painting, along with two portraits
of Madruzzo's nephews painted by
Gian Battista Moroni, belonged to the
Castello del Buon Consiglio, Trent,
and were mentioned in an inventory of 1599.
With the extinction of the Madruzzo
family in 1658, the paintings were inherited
by the Roccabruna family, of Trent, whose
last descendant, in 1735, left them to
the Barons Guadenti della Torre.
From them, they passed to the
Baron Valentino di Salvatori, also in
Trent. This canvas was taken to Paris
in 1907 and acquired on the art market
by James Stillman, New York.
In the Museum since 1951.
At left, a detail.

JACOPO TINTORETTO. *Ecce Homo.*

Although this work unquestionably belongs to his early period—a Tintoretto who has not yet forgotten the lessons of Titian—the canvas already reveals the characteristic style of the master. The typical composition on the diagonal, the chiaroscuro contrasts, and the serpentine reflections of light in the folds of the clothing are elements which were to mature and to intensify in later works. The profoundly dramatic scene unfolds among the crowd compressed at the left beneath the tempestuous sky, and spreading to the two apostles Peter and John frightened by pain on the first step of the staircase, culminates at the top in the luminous figure of Jesus between Pilate and his lieutenant. The figure on foot, at the left, in purple and yellow, seems to be instigating the yet undecided crowd to cry out the word "Crucify!" which was to carry the Redeemer to Calvary. The detail of the dog lying on the step, unaware of the immensity of the tragedy developing around him, is very moving.

32

TINTORETTO (JACOPO ROBUSTI)
Venice, c. 1518-Venice 1594.
Ecce Homo (c. 1547)
Oil on canvas, 109 x 136 cm.
From the gallery of the Marchesi Gonzaga, Mantua, the painting was sold in England in the seventeenth century. It later belonged to the Sedelmeyer Collection, Paris.
In the Museum since 1949.

AGNOLO BRONZINO. *Portrait of a Young Nobleman.*

Owing to its evident inferiority in comparison with other works by Bronzino, the critic A. McComb advanced the hypothesis that this portrait might be by his contemporary Francesco Salviati. In any case, it is a typical example of Mannerist academicism, with abstract immobility and inexpressive coldness, under arbitrary lighting. The showy lace collar is another example of the artist's academic pedantry in the execution of details.

PARIS BORDONE. *A member of the Contarini Family.*

Although less controlled and more superficial than Titian, his pupil Paris Bordone was able in this canvas to characterize with penetration the skeptical and proud expression of this rich merchant, who flaunts gloves, a fur-lined pelisse, and a mysterious little box, perhaps full of jewels.

CARLO SARACENI
Venice 1580-Venice 1620
Venus and Mars (1605–1610)
Oil on copper; 39 x 52 cm.
In the Museum since 1947.

CARLO SARACENI. *Venus and Mars.*

This small oil, which was at one time attributed to one of the Northern masters working in Rome at the beginning of the seventeenth century and most recently was judged by Longhi to have been painted by Saraceni, illustrates the familiar myth of the love of Venus and Mars. Here we see a pompous background of conventional trees and hills, curtains flowing in the wind and amorettos dancing around the god's armor.

PIETRO DA CORTONA
Cortona 1596-Rome 1669
Moses and Jethro's Daughters
Oil on canvas; 123 x 169 cm.
From the collection of the
Marchese Carlo Lotteringhi della Stufa,
Florence. It was one of the paintings
chosen to represent Pietro da Cortona
in the exhibition of "*Pittura italiana
del '600 e '700,*" *in Florence in 1922.*
In the Museum since 1948.

PIETRO DA CORTONA. *Moses and Jethro's Daughters.* *p. 34*

In this magnificent canvas, rich in movement and effects of chiaroscuro inspired by the style of Tintoretto, the Cortona master narrates Moses' adventure while a refugee in the land of Midian. He drove away the shepherds who were threatening Jethro's seven daughters while they were getting water to give to their father's sheep. Upon moving to Rome in 1616, Pietro da Cortona was greatly impressed by the frescoes of Raphael and Michelangelo and by Bernini's dynamic sculptures. His famous frescoes in the Barberini Palace in Rome and in the Pitti Palace in Florence establish him as one of the great exponents of Baroque mural painting.

FOLLOWER OF GIOVANNI LORENZO BERNINI. *Diana Sleeping.*

This statue is presently exhibited in the Museum on a Roman sarcophagus which depicts the story of Meleager. It is mentioned by the eighteenth-century French traveler Charles de Brosses in his *Lettres Familières.* He saw it in 1740 at the Barberini Palace in Rome, attributed to Bernini along with some imitations of classical sculptures which the prince of the Baroque never attempted. Traditionally attributed to Bernini, perhaps owing to the grace of some of the details—such as the hair bound with ribbons which is reminiscent of his *Daphne*—this marble statue was considered a work of Bernini's youth and later as one of his late maturity. Yet it still cannot be included in a Bernini catalogue. It should be considered the work of a valiant sculptor of several decades later, who foreshadows eighteenth-century styles. Indeed, the classical flavor of Diana gives the impression of a composition imitative of several fragments from antiquity; it is a poetic work in a style which became greatly in favor in Italy in the early eighteenth century.

**FOLLOWER OF GIOVANNI
LORENZO BERNINI**
Naples 1598-Rome 1680
Diana Sleeping
Marble; 169 cm. long.
From the Barberini Palace, Rome.
Excluded from the *fideicommissum* between
the Barberini princes and the
Italian government, it was acquired
by the Museum in 1950.

36

JACOPO PALMA THE YOUNGER
Venice 1544 - Venice 1628
A Patriarch of Venice
Oil on canvas, 352 x 210 cm.
Signed and dated in 1620; inscription:
JACOPUS PALMA DE ROBORE SUMPSIT.
In the Museum since 1947.

GUIDO RENI
Bologna 1575-Bologna 1642
Lucretia
Oil on canvas; 113 x 90 cm.
Belonged traditionally to
Cardinal Mazarin and remained until
his death in his private palace in
Paris, which today is the seat of the
French Institute. A fire there in 1660
was probably responsible for the darkening
of the varnishes. This defect was recently
corrected in a restoration which took place
at the Museum. The painting is from the
collection of the Lubomirski prince,
who donated it to the Museum in 1959.

JACOPO PALMA THE YOUNGER. *A Patriarch of Venice.* *p. 36*

The inscription of the legend, *Jacopus Palma de robore sumpsit,* seems to indicate that the Venetian painter "took upon himself" to finish an uncompleted canvas by a "stronger" master, while conserving the initial scheme.

GUIDO RENI. *Lucretia.*

Languid, sweet, and sentimental, this representation of the Roman matron, wife of Lucius Tarquinius Collatinus, is one of the many "Lucretias" painted by the much discussed Bolognese painter. Reni, who consistently tended towards an affected and declamatory style, chromatically cold and conventional, managed in his final phase, to reveal a vigorous search for form.

37

GIOVANNI BATTISTA PITTONI. *Bacchus and Ariadne.*

This canvas describes the myth of Ariadne. Bacchus discovers her on the island of Naxos after she had been abandoned by Theseus, and marries her. In contrast to the excessive polychromy of Bacchus and the satyrs, the woman stands out graciously in a delicate harmony of whites, yellows and pinks, recalling the feminine figures of Titian and Tintoretto.

GIOVANNI ANTONIO PELLEGRINI. *Queen Thomyris.*

The components of this and other paintings by Pellegrini are a tonal fluidity and chromatic sweetness, manipulated in a light, sparkling and delicate manner. For this imaginative and exuberant artist, the name of the mythical queen was a simple pretext to portray a smiling Venetian lady. He contrasts the cold, metallic hardness of the helmet with the softness of breasts and arms, exhibited with the open nonchalance of seventeenth-century women.

VALERIO VILLAREALE. *Sleeping Bacchante.* *p. 39*

Villareale was a neoclassical sculptor and archaeologist who participated in the excavations in Syracuse. He made large decorations in stucco, which was the traditional technique of Sicily; his Sala de Astrea in the Royal Palace of Caserta should be remembered. Villareale also carved statues in a neo-Hellenistic style, such as this Bacchante asleep on a leopard skin.

GIOVANNI BATTISTA PITTONI
Venice 1687-Venice 1767
Bacchus and Ariadne (c. 1733)
There exists a version of this
painting in the Brera Museum, Milan.
Oil on canvas; 72 x 53 cm.
In the Museum since 1949.

GIOVANNI ANTONIO PELLEGRINI
Venice 1675-Venice 1741
Queen Thomyris (c. 1720–1725)
Oil on canvas; 123 x 97 cm.
In the Museum since 1947.

ALESSANDRO MAGNASCO. *Landscape with Shepherds and a Hermit.*

The two fundamental themes of Magnasco are found together in this seductive canvas: the open, luminous landscapes and the closed mysterious penumbras filled with spectral figures. Thelandscape here is constructed through placing into contrast the spectacular verticality of the trees and the horizontal flight of the clouds above the distant horizon.

GAETANO PREVIATI. *Landscape.* *p. 40*

This is a simple document of diaphanous and uneven divisionism, typical of the Ferrarese painter Previati, who was more a theoretician than a master of this technique.

GAETANO PREVIATI
Ferrara 1852-Lavagna 1920
Landscape
Oil on canvas; 86 x 117 cm.
Signed at lower left:
Previati.
In the Museum since 1949.

GIOVANNI BOLDINI. *The Poet Hanvin.*

Another painter from Ferrara, who was living in Paris, Boldini was well known for his ability to quickly capture and immediately characterize his sitters in the style of Frans Hals. His portraits of late-century Parisian personalities, such as this elegant Parnassian poet, reveal another side of the Bohemian life of Montmartre.

FILIPPO DE PISIS. *Portrait.*

This canvas belongs to the expressionist phase of this metaphysical painter who from his early Futurist experiences gradually arrived at a painting which was rich in chromatic sonorities, like those of a Guardi.

GIOVANNI BOLDINI
Ferrara 1845-Paris 1931
The Poet Hanvin (c. 1890)
Oil on panel; 48 x 24 cm.
In the Museum since 1947.

FILIPPO DE PISIS
Ferrara 1896-Monza 1955
Portrait
Oil on cardboard; 69 x 53 cm.
Signed and dated at lower right:
de Pisis 1928.
In the Museum since 1951.

FRANCE AND
THE SCHOOL OF PARIS

The collection of French art is the most important section of the Museum. The reason for this lies in the history of Brazil, where French culture has always been present and generally accepted. Without taking into account the Calvinistic colonial adventures of Admiral Villegaignon in the sixteenth century and the attempts by pirates to implant French stations on the Atlantic coast in the seventeenth century, by the eighteenth century—in spite of the tight Portuguese rule—the influence of the French Encyclopedists, of the Revolution, and later of Romanticism penetrated Brazil. As a result of the Napoleonic conquests, the Portuguese royal family took shelter in Rio de Janeiro. With the aim of building a capital and introducing a cultural life, King John VI—instead of showing resentment toward the Bonaparte invaders of his country—appealed to France. A cultural mission led by Joachim Le Breton, Secretary of the Section of Fine Arts of the French Institute, and composed of an architect, painters, sculptors, and artisans arrived in Rio de Janeiro in 1816 and founded the Academy, thus inaugurating Parisian customs and manners—as far as circumstances would allow. While commerce was being consolidated in the hands of the English, the literary and journalistic movements, the budding of philosophy, the intellectual climate, and more than anything else the plastic arts found their expression in French patterns. Throughout the whole nineteenth century, with the exception of some sporadic flirtations with Germany, Brazilian culture depended on Paris. The Brazilian Romantic poets founded their magazine *Nictheroy* there; the most important Brazilian publisher was a branch of the Parisian Garnier; the goal of national artists was the *Ville-lumière;* theatres were built with the image of the *Opéra* in mind; the wealthy plantation owners spent their vacations in Paris and returned with large quantities of decorative objects. Santos-Dumont confirmed his aeronautical inventions by flying around the Eiffel Tower. Relations with France became increasingly closer. Brazilian poetry would be Hugoan, Parnassian, Decadent, whatever the French was, subject to a time lag in its arrival. The Brazilian cultural development, although derived from the Portuguese who gave the country its language, is substantially French. The founder of the Museum, who in his youth had been a Professor of Roman Law at the University of Recife— which was still under the influence of the romantic Germanophile Tobias Barreto—displayed a natural liking for France. The cultural presence of France never diminished in intensity. Just before Brazil entered the First World War, the French ambassador in Rio de Janeiro was Paul Claudel, assisted by the composer Darius Milhaud, both of whom deliberately contributed to strengthening the spiritual links with France in our universities already full of professors from the Sorbonne. All this contributed to the Museum's cultural awareness of France, not to mention the offerings and support which so cordially and plentifully came from the Parisian art dealer Georges Wildenstein and his son Daniel. The collection ought to be seen as a reflection of these circumstances.

FRANÇOIS CLOUET. *The Bath of Diana.*

This masterpiece of French painting is an unusual theme for the famous son of Jean Clouet. He was generally more occupied in producing portraits, such as those of the botanist Pierre Cutte, Henry II, and Elizabeth of Austria. The panel, which has been studied exhaustively by the French art historian René Huyghe, evidences Clouet's contribution to the formation of solidity and realism in the Fontainebleau School. This occurred upon the arrival of some of the outstanding personalities of Italian Mannerism, who replaced the linear play of shapes with a type of trompe-l'oeil rich in depth, relief and spatiality. In this painting Clouet inaugurates a theme which was to have constant success in the following centuries and culminate in the *fêtes galantes* of Watteau and Lancret. This is probably the prototype version, of which there are variants in the Rouen Museum and in the Sulzbach Collection, Paris. The subject is an allusion to the love affair of Henry II— who appears on the horse—and Diane de Poitiers. In the other versions, the principal characters are respectively Charles IX and Marie Touchet, Henry IV and Gabrielle d'Estrées.

FRANÇOIS CLOUET
Tours, c. 1505-Paris 1572
The Bath of Diana (c. 1545)
Oil on panel; 78 x 110 cm.
From the Neher Collection, Paris.
In the Museum since 1953.

43

NICOLAS POUSSIN
Les Andelys (Normandy) 1594-Rome 1665
Floral Offering at a Marriage Feast,
or *Dance in Honor of Priapus*
(c. 1637)
Oil on canvas: 167 x 376 cm.
Detail, page 46.

45

NICOLAS POUSSIN. *Floral Offering at a Marriage Feast.*   *p. 44–46*

In his catalogue-raisonné of Poussin's works, Sir Anthony Blunt titled this painting "Dance in Honor of Priapus." He indicated that the painter, while planning this work, was inspired by one of Marliano's engravings, *Topographia antiquae urbis Roma,* and only omitted the sacrifice of the ass, which was a fundamental scene in the offerings to Priapus. In keeping with Roman bas-reliefs, which Poussin had studied in detail, the immense panel follows a rigorous horizontality, interrupted only by the woman kneeling down in front of the statue, and by the beautiful female figure at the extreme right who observes the bacchanal with smiling irony.

JEAN-MARC NATTIER. *The Princesses of France.*   *p. 47*

Nattier was a sophisticated painter of fashionable women. Making allusions to their natural features, he mixes undeniable bravura with the art of re-

JEAN-MARC NATTIER
Paris 1685-Paris 1766
The Princesses of France:
Madame Adélaide as Air;
Madame Henriette as Fire;
Madame Louise-Elisabeth as Earth;
Madame Victoire as Water.
Oils on canvas; 106 x 138 cm, each.
Signed and dated:
Nattier pinxit 1751.
Belonged to the Palace of Versailles until
the contents were auctioned after the French
Revolution; then entered the collection
of Baron Robert de Rothschild, Paris.
In the Museum since 1952.
Facing page: Madame Henriette (above)
Adélaide, detail (lower left);
Louise-Elisabeth, detail (lower center);
Victoire, detail (lower right).

fined flattery. He corrects, improves, and rearranges coiffures; he colors hair and faces; he adorns his models with silks and velvets. Yet his tonal harmonies and compositional rhythms are agreeable, particularly in the portrait of Madame Henriette sitting beside the flaming symbol of her feminine charm.

48

JEAN-BAPTISTE PATER
Valenciennes 1695-Paris 1736
Meeting in a Park (c. 1730)
Oil on canvas; 65 x 81 cm.
Signed on the rock, at bottom:
Pater.
Formerly in the collection of Frederick
the Great, and kept in the New Palace in
Potsdam until it was sold by Emperor
William II to the Wildenstein family, Paris.
In the Museum since 1953.

FRANÇOIS LE MOINE
Paris 1688-Paris 1737
Picnic during the Hunt
Oil on canvas; 223 x 185 cm.
Signed and dated on the rock:
F. Le Moine 1723.
From the Collection of Lord
Rosebery, London. Donated to the Museum
by Georges Wildenstein in 1958.

FRANÇOIS LE MOINE.   *Picnic during the Hunt.*   p. 48

This festive scene is an outstanding work of Rococo painting. The warmth
and gaiety of the colors, the atmospheric luminosity, and the compositional
verve, all are reminiscent of Lancret's *Fêtes galantes.* The art historian Cor-
rado Ricci has called attention to the influence of the Venetian *vedutisti* in
the works of Le Moine.

JEAN-BAPTISTE PATER.   *Meeting in a Park.*

A contemporary of Watteau, as is Le Moine, Pater was a specialist in imag-
ining his themes through the scenes and anecdotes of *fêtes galantes.* This
resourceful painter composes one of his frivolous and elegant minuets
through colors which are transparent and softened by shadings and precios-
ities.

49

JEAN-BAPTISTE-SIMÉON CHARDIN. *Portrait of
Auguste-Gabriel Godefroy.*

Simple, allusive, and profoundly honest—far from the corrupt and libertine
world of Versailles—Chardin paints objects and family figures in the intimacy of their home: women engaged in household tasks, playing music
boxes or serving chocolate; young boys drawing or playing shuttlecock or
with a top, as in this portrait of one of the sons of the jeweler Godefroy, his

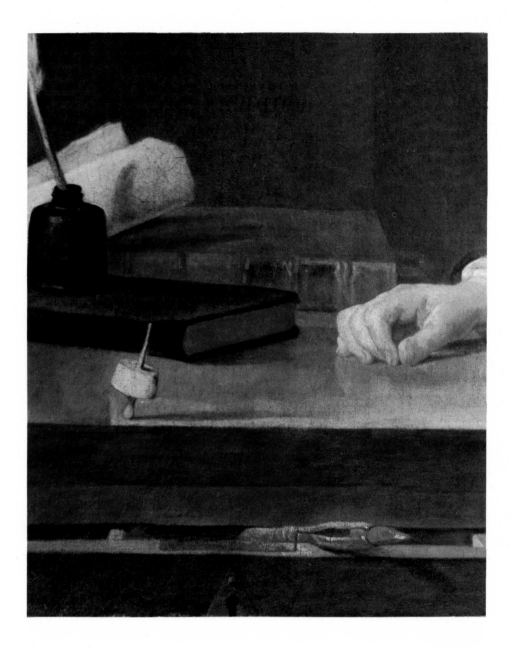

JEAN-BAPTISTE-SIMÉON CHARDIN
Paris 1699-Paris 1779
Portrait of Auguste-Gabriel Godefroy
Oil on canvas: 67 x 73 cm.
Signed and dated in center:
Chardin 1741.
Mentioned in sale catalogue
of Chevalier Antonio de la Roque,
Paris, 1745. A century later, appeared
in the sale of Marquis de Cypierre;
later in that of the Marquis de Montesquieu.
There is a version of the painting
in the Louvre Museum, Paris.
Detail at right.
In the Museum since 1958.

friend. In these people, he recognized his own special world, just like Vermeer, although so different in technique. In contrast to Vermeer, Chardin prefers the tonalities that emerge from darkness rather than those that shine in full light. His chromatic texture is a closed and vibrant web of entwining gradations with rapid strokes rather than one made up of ample surfaces. His best canvases are his still-lifes, which he turned to when his vision began to fail at about forty years of age. Seated before his easel, smoking a small earthenware pipe, and looking over the top of his glasses, he fixedly observed simple objects: jugs, cups, bread, fruit, game. He looked at them from a detached point of view, disregarding objective details in order to reap their plastic values, which he chromatically translated into majestic harmonies.

51

FRANÇOIS-HUBERT DROUAIS. *The Duke of Berry and the Count of Provence as Children.*

The virtuoso Drouais, a pupil of Jean Baptiste Vanloo, meets the requirements for a court painter in this meticulously detailed painting. The work is complemented by sumptuous accessories, including mechanical reproduction and perfect resemblance, as if reflected in a mirror. These are the reverential images of two children who would later become kings of France: the Duke of Berry as Louis XVI, beheaded at the Revolution; and the Count of Provence as Louis XVIII, who reigned after the fall of Napoleon.

JEAN-ANTOINE HOUDON. *Voltaire.* *p. 53.*

Houdon portrayed Voltaire a number of times. In this marble, he was able to capture with great naturalness the shrewd and mordant mask of the eminent essayist and philosopher of the Enlightenment, the caustic harasser of tyrants, fanatics, superstitious ignorance and impenitent optimists.

FRANÇOIS-HUBERT DROUAIS
Paris 1727-Paris 1775
*The Duke of Berry and
the Count of Provence as Children*
Oil on canvas; 95 x 127 cm.
Signed and dated, on the base
of the vase at the left:
Drouais, le fils 1757.
In the collection of
Versailles Palace until the French
Revolution, when it was exported.
It later appeared in the Burdett-Coutts
Collection, London.
In the Museum since 1954.

JEAN-ANTOINE HOUDON
Versailles 1741-Paris 1828
Voltaire
Marble; height 47 cm.
Signed and dated, on the base:
Voltaire; Houdon 1778 Sculpsit.
Originally belonged to Voltaire's granddaughter,
Madame Dompierre d'Hornoy, who received it
directly from the philosopher. It was then
given to her sister, Mme. Denis, afterwards
belonged to her heir, M. de Vaudeul. It was
acquired, at the end of the last century,
by Eduardo Guinle, in Paris. His son
Guilherme donated it to the Museum in 1958.

JEAN-HONORÉ FRAGONARD.   *Education is Everything.*

This painting was discovered by Boucher, who took it to his atelier. Until the fall of Louis XVI, Fragonard was a brilliant painter of voluptuous subjects, sensual allegories based on mythological themes. He combined in his canvases the impetuosity of Rubens and the meditated coloring of Rembrandt, both of whom he greatly admired. The outbreak of the Revolution and the appearance of David put an end to this libertine painting. When he was about forty, Fragonard married an eighteen year-old student and his palette became more homespun and kind. The atelier was inhabited by children and animals. *Education is Everything* is one of his first paintings with a moral message.

JEAN-HONORÉ FRAGONARD
Grasse 1732-Paris 1806
Education is Everything. (c. 1780)
Oil on canvas; 56 x 66 cm.
Originally belonged to M. Aubert, Paris;
sold in 1786; then belonged to Nicolas
de Launay, who engraved it with its pendant,
The Little Preacher, which was also in
his possession, and appeared on sale
in 1792. Later in the collection of
Baron H. Thyssen-Bornemisza, Lugano.
In the Museum since 1958.

JEAN-AUGUSTE-DOMINIQUE INGRES. *Angelica Chained.*

JEAN-AUGUSTE-DOMINIQUE INGRES
Montauban 1780-Paris 1867
Angelica Chained
Oil on canvas; 97 x 75 cm.
Signed and dated:
J. Ingres 1859.
Inscribed on back of canvas:
*Ce Tableau, première pensée de
l'Angélique, executé en 1818, a été
terminé sur ma demande et pour moi par
Monsieur Ingres en 1859 Haro*
Belonged to Étienne-François
Haro, Ingres' dealer.
In the Museum since 1958.

This oil depicting Ariosto's heroine chained to a reef on a fanciful island, waiting to be devoured by a sea monster, is part of a series of preliminary studies for the painting *Ruggiero Freeing Angelica,* in the Louvre. Although Ingres in his youth painted some soberly constructed portraits, he fell into heavy academicism in this study, mixing verism and affected sentimentalism, as a result of his prolonged contact with the remnants of classicism during his almost twenty years in Rome and Florence. Meanwhile, the new wave of Romanticism led by Delacroix was revolutionizing French painting.

55

CAMILLE COROT
Paris 1796-Paris 1875
Roses in a Glass
Oil on canvas;
32.5 x 24.5 cm.
Signed and dated at lower right:
COROT Juin 1874.
Given by Corot as a gift to a friend.
Passed through the collection
of Bernheim-Jeune, Paris;
then finally to Gaston Bernheim
de Villers, Paris.
In the Museum since 1952.

CAMILLE COROT
Paris 1796-Paris 1875
Portrait of Laurent-Denis Sennegon
Oil on canvas; 40 x 34 cm.
Signed and dated at lower right:
C. COROT 1842.
Belonged to Corot until his death,
then passed through several collections.
In the Museum since 1951.

CAMILLE COROT. *Gypsy with Mandolin.* *p. 57*

Corot's portraits, just like his landscapes, are pictorial transpositions of the states of the soul. Delicate hues and a soft luminosity permeate his images, which have a sense of solid construction. Corot, who was a lover of nature and human beings, like all lovers idealizes the creatures he observes. Braque, who was a great admirer of Corot, painted an interpretation of this work with tonalities of pleasing intimacy as an homage to the master.

CAMILLE COROT. *Portrait of Laurent-Denis Sennegon.*

Corot had a special affection for his family, twelve members of whom are known from portraits he painted. This one is of his brother-in-law Sennegon, who was married to Annette-Octavie, one of the painter's three sisters.

CAMILLE COROT. *Roses in a Glass.*

At 78, just one year prior to his death, in the silent melancholy of old age, the good "*père Corot*" still was able to paint this little jewel, which manages to illuminate the tired eyes of the old master through its flash of white and red.

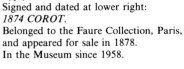

CAMILLE COROT
Gypsy with Mandolin
Signed and dated at lower right:
1874 COROT.
Belonged to the Faure Collection, Paris,
and appeared for sale in 1878.
In the Museum since 1958.

At left: Georges Braque:
Hommage à Corot, 1922,
National Museum of Modern Art, Paris.

HONORÉ DAUMIER. *Two Heads.* p. 58

Daumier, Goya's most worthy successor, possessed the robust qualities of a painter, although his contemporaries almost exclusively admired him as a caricaturist. Although he suffered the inevitable consequences of his habitual black and white graphic technique, this small oil is constructed with thick yellow, red and brown brushstrokes, aiming to achieve a sober and powerful harmony by using a few essential tonalities in a masterfully handled tormented context.

HONORÉ DAUMIER
Marseilles 1808-Paris 1879
Two Heads (1857-1862)
Oil on cardboard; 23 x 30 cm.
Initialed at lower left: *h d*
From the Démetelle Collection, Paris.
Identified by J. Adhémar
as number 45 or 47 in the *Exposition des
peintures et dessins de H. Daumier,*
Durand-Ruel Gallery, Paris, 1878.
In the Museum since 1958.

Facing page
EUGÈNE DELACROIX
Winter: Juno Imploring Aeolus

HONORÉ DAUMIER
The Fugitives
Plaster; 35 x 75 cm.
Signed at lower right:
H. Daumier.
From the Atelier Daumier.
Of this plaster there exist
a preparatory design,
a version in terracotta, and two
castings in bronze done around 1880.
Donated to the Museum by
Georges Wildenstein in 1958.

HONORÉ DAUMIER. *The Fugitives.*

Another aspect of the multifaceted Daumier is revealed by this plaster in its stone-like modelling and the sense of human comprehension that always constituted the fundamental impulse of the great master from Marseilles.

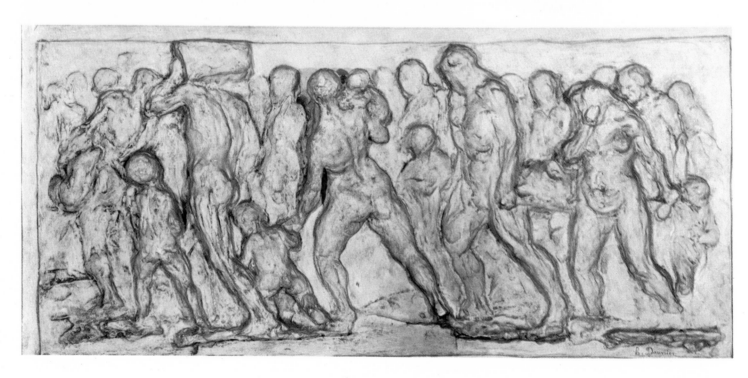

Spring:
Eurydice Gathering Flowers

Summer:
Diana Surprised by Actaeon

Autumn:
Bacchus Meets Ariadne

EUGÈNE DELACROIX
Charenton-Meurice,
Paris 1798-Paris 1863
The Four Seasons (1856-1861)

Spring:
Eurydice Gathering Flowers

Summer:
Diana Surprised by Actaeon

Autumn:
Bacchus Meets Ariadne

Winter:
Juno Imploring Aeolus,
Page 59

Oils on canvas,
196 x 166 cm. each.
Commissioned in 1856 by the Alsatian
banker Frédéric Hartmann, but
remained in the Delacroix's
studio until his death.
The dealer Haro acquired them in the
Delacroix sale in 1864 and after
having been in several collections,
they passed to Durand-Ruel, Paris.
In the Museum since 1951.

EUGÈNE DELACROIX. *The Four Seasons.* p. 59–60.

These four canvases, interrupted by the death of the painter in 1863, were "finished" at the end of the century by a mediocre academic painter, but later restored to their initial freshness. Perhaps owing to the fact that they remained unfinished, they reveal with greater clarity the compositional dynamism and chromatic nervousness with which Delacroix constructed his paintings; he aimed above all to achieve what he called the *musique du tableau,* that magical harmony of lines and colors which captures the eye before one realizes what the painting represents.

GUSTAVE COURBET. *Zélie Courbet* and *Juliette Courbet.*

The master of Realism painted his sisters several times. The portrait of Zélie, which is unique in Courbet's pictorial language, admirably fuses the tenderness and moral strength of a woman who was "... always ill, always courageous, always pleasant ..." The portrait of Juliette, the youngest of the family, is more romantic. The sweet, small, pensive face emerges majestically from the dark mass of the dress, and is rhythmically set off by the pink-white sequence of the cuff, the hand, and the collar.

ADOLPHE-JOSEPH-THOMAS
MONTICELLI
Marseilles 1824-Marseilles 1886
Imaginary Village
Oil on canvas: 28 x 38 cm.
From the Goupil Gallery, Paris,
where it was exhibited in 1918.
In the Museum since 1950.

ADOLPHE-JOSEPH-THOMAS MONTICELLI. *Imaginary Village.*

In this marine landscape, probably of the outskirts of Marseilles, the painter spells out the forms, syllable by syllable, spreading his colors with the violent impastos that were unique to him, almost like a magician of painting. Van Gogh expressed great admiration for him because he felt him to be a brother in his almost insane effort at the easel, "... when the spirit is extremely tense, like an actor in a difficult role, obliged to think about a thousand things at the same moment."

ANTOINE VOLLON
Lyon 1833-Paris 1900
Still Life
Oil on canvas; 81 x 117 cm.
Signed at lower left:
A. Vollon
From the Chester Dale Collection,
donated by him to the Museum in 1951.

ÉDOUARD MANET
Paris 1832-Paris 1883
Pertuiset, Lion Hunter
Oil on canvas; 150 x 170 cm.
Signed and dated on the tree trunk:
Manet 1881
From the Pertuiset Collection passed
to several German collections.
In the Museum since 1950.

ANTOINE VOLLON. *Still Life.*   *p. 62*

This minutely finished and artificially composed still life is typical of the
mid-nineteenth-century French academic manner, which was quite successful in its time and influenced a number of Brazilian artists studying in Paris.

ÉDOUARD MANET. *Pertuiset, Lion Hunter.*

The model for this tartarinesque Nimrod was a good friend of Manet, a dil-
ettante painter and inveterate hunter, who enjoyed himself by putting on
imaginary safaris in his garden in Montmartre and shooting a lion's skin
instead of rabbits. In addition to being a way of making fun of his friend,
this painting served as a pretext for a plein-air study, in Manet's noncon-
formist manner. It shocked the bourgeoisie of the period, who could only
appreciate a "photographic" reproduction of reality.   63

ÉDOUARD MANET
The Artist, or *Portrait of*
Gilbert-Marcellin Desboutin
Oil on canvas; 191 x 130 cm.
Signed and dated at lower right:
Manet 1875.
Sold by Manet to Hubert Debrousse,
and exhibited in a posthumous
exhibition of Manet's works in 1884.

In 1900, acquired by Auguste Pellerin
at the Exposition Universelle, and appeared
as part of his collection at the Bernheim-
Jeune Gallery, Paris. The painting then made
its way to Germany, where it was bought
by Eduard Arnhold, along with the *Famille*
Monet dans le Jardin, for three hundred
thousand francs.
In the Museum since 1954.

65

ÉDOUARD MANET.   *The Artist.*   p. 64–65

Manet was the target for the sarcasms of contemporary critics. This painting, "... black from one end to the other like a portrait of a coal miner
...," is a portrait of the painter and poet Gilbert-Marcellin Desboutin, an
eccentric figure of the bohemian life of Paris. What we can admire in it is
the ability with which Manet confronted the problem of harmonizing the
somber bluish-green hues of black against black, enhancing the strange noc-
turnal apparition.

ÉDOUARD MANET.   *The Horsewoman.*

This painting of Mme. Lefébure is one of the two equestrian portraits painted by Manet; the other is *Gentleman,* done in the same year. Painted for his
own pleasure, at a time when he was continually being rejected at the official expositions, this oil marks a phase of the revolution which Manet was
carrying out in search of new relationships between colors and surfaces
66   through a unidimensional colorism.

ÉDOUARD MANET
The Horsewoman (1875)
Oil on canvas; 90 x 116 cm.
Signed (by his widow after the
painter's death) at lower right:
Certifié d'Ed. Manet Mme Manet.
In the Museum since 1958.

ÉDOUARD MANET
Bathers on the Seine
Oil on canvas; 132 x 98 cm.
From the collection of
Auguste Pellerin, Paris.
In the Museum since 1951.

ÉDOUARD MANET. *Bathers on the Seine.*

Although this painting was never completed, it is perfectly finished as regards the harmony between the clarity of the nudes and the luminous shadows of the background, against which the two bathers rhythmically stand out. One can note in this canvas—which already possesses the spontaneous freshness of his later works—an interesting change of mind on the part of the artist. He repainted the right leg of the principal figure in a more bent position and thus gained greater movement in contrast to the immobility of the rock.

67

EDGAR-HILAIRE-GERMAIN DEGAS. *Woman Drying Herself.*
Four Ballerinas on stage.   *p. 69*

Degas, obsessed by the sensation of forms in movement, at the racetrack, at
the theatres, at the circus, at the ballet, pursued untiringly the suggestion he
had received as a youngster from Ingres: "Make lines, lots of lines, either
from memory, or from nature." With his famous dancers and women at the
bath, which were sketched rapidly under the sharp lights of the stage or in
the intimacy of the studio, and through the use of soft pastels, he created
luminous and suggestive images which are rich in their plastic elements and
human allusions.

EDGAR-HILAIRE-GERMAIN DEGAS
Paris 1834-Paris 1917
Woman Drying Herself
Charcoal and pastel on paper; 61 x 51 cm.
In the collection of Dr. Robyn, Brussels.
In the Museum since 1954.

EDGAR-HILAIRE-GERMAIN DEGAS
Four Dancers on Stage
(c. 1892). Signed at lower right:
Degas.
Remained in the artist's studio until
his death and appeared in the first Degas
sale, Georges Petit Gallery, Paris, 1918.
Then acquired by the Barnes Foundation,
Merion, Pa.,
and appeared on the New York market
after World War II.
In the Museum since 1950.

EDGAR-HILAIRE-GERMAIN DEGAS. *Bronzes.*   *p. 71–75*

The Museum possesses seventy-three bronzes by Degas, all acquired in 1951. They are exhibited in rotation in the Museum and are divided by thematic groups, with the exception of the *Fourteen-Year-Old Ballerina,* which is placed with two of the master's pastels and an oil painting. Whenever the whole collection is exhibited, such as when the Museum was completely given over to its French holdings, the spectacle is sensational. Such occasions recall the reservations of the artist who said: "It is too great a responsibility to leave behind something in bronze, the material is eternal." Degas, the most constructive personality of the nineteenth century, was taken with sensations and experiences of form obtained in all techniques, which is evident in the multiplicity of female nude contortionists and horses in violent motion. Degas appeared to be the inheritor of Ingres' formula. Each figure in movement or in repose after movement is characterized by an animal-like individualism, by its humanness without symbolism, by cruelty, by a "... special tone of scorn and hatred ...". These characteristics have earned for him the reputation of being a misogynist; yet he was a timid, solitary, almost ascetic man. The poetic pathos of a back-to-nature realism possessed him, but with new visionary aims. It is a wonder to imagine the clay modeled by his hands, which obeyed only tactile reflexes because in his old age blindness claimed his ability to play with light. An extremely astute analyzer and harmonizer, he on one occasion told Vollard that one *Dancer* was in her twentieth transformation: "This time, I have it." But he ended up destroying her "... for the pleasure of beginning again."

The stubborn beliefs of the sculptor Degas are of such amplitude that they go beyond definition, although they agree perfectly with comparisons that have been made between the artist as embodying and reviving the spirit of the Renaissance and the protagonist Michelangelo.

The statue *Fourteen Year-Old Ballerina* was noted in the Catalogue of the Impressionist Exhibition of 1880, but it was actually only shown in the following year. The original wax is in the Louvre. The preparatory drawings are conserved in the Doucet Library, Paris, and are reproduced in John Rewald's catalogue of Degas' sculptures. The most penetrating description of the work is due to Louis Gillet: "... with her pug-nosed face and her knock-kneed legs, her immature, acid, angular, irritating forms, in her grace as an idol and as a ghost, trivial as a street urchin and yet, austere, hierarchical and cloistered, like a millennial Isis in the temples of Memphis and Luxor."

EDGAR-HILAIRE-GERMAIN DEGAS
Fourteen-Year-Old Dancer (1880)
Bronze, partially painted; muslin
skirt (*tutu bouffant*) and original lace;
height 99 cm.
Acquired with the Degas bronze
collection, on the
London art market in 1951.

EDGAR-HILAIRE-GERMAIN DEGAS
Dancer at Rest, height 37.5 cm;
Dancer at Rest, height 44.5 cm;
Great Arabesque, First Time,
height 48 cm.
At left: *Dancer with Castanets*,
height 27.5 cm.

EDGAR-HILAIRE-GERMAIN DEGAS
Fourth Position Front,
on the Left Leg, height 57 cm.
Dancer with Castanets,
height 27.5cm.
Spanish Dance, height 40.5 cm;
Spanish Dance, height 45 cm;
At right: *Spanish Dance,* height 40.5 cm.

EDGAR-HILAIRE-GERMAIN DEGAS
Seated Woman Drying Herself
on the Left Side
Bronze, height 35 cm.

EDGAR-HILAIRE-GERMAIN DEGAS
Study for the
Fourteen-Year-Old Dancer
Bronze, height 72 cm.

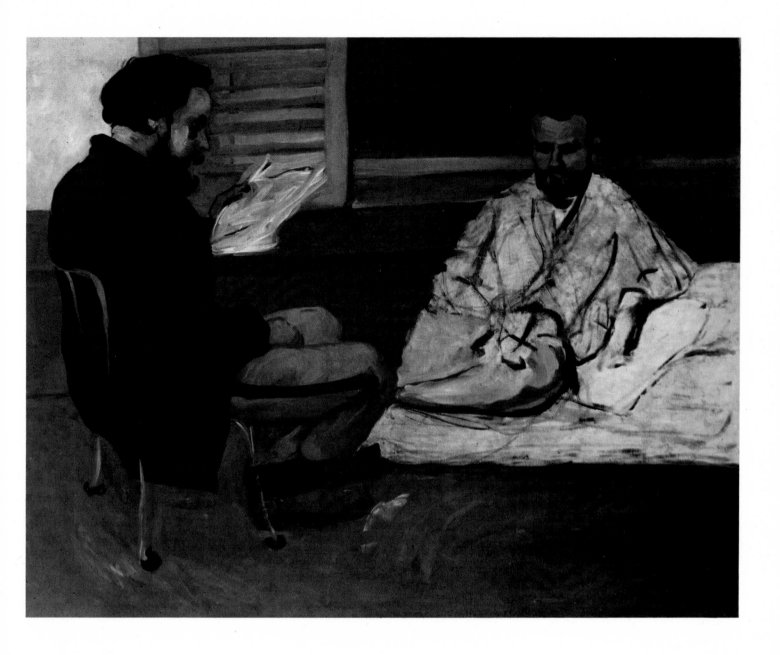

PAUL CÉZANNE
Paul Alexis Reading a Manuscript to Zola
(1869–1870)
Oil on canvas; 130 x 160 cm.
Found in 1927 in the basement of Zola's
home in Médan by his widow. Passed to
the collection of J. Pellerin, Paris.
In the Museum since 1951.

PAUL CÉZANNE
Aix-en-Provence 1839-
Aix-en-Provence 1906
The Negro Scipion (c. 1866)
Oil on canvas; 107 x 83 cm.
Given by Zola to Monet as a present;
remained in Monet's atelier
in Giverny until his death. Through
the Brazilian ambassador Jayme de Barros,
sold to the Museum by Michel Monet,
the master's son, in 1950.

Paul CÉZANNE. *The Negro Scipion.* *p. 76*

Scipion was a popular model in Paris. He posed principally at the "Acadé-mie Suisse," which Cézanne frequented between 1865 and 1870. This work belongs to his transitional phase in which the painter was still preoccupied with the effects of chiaroscuro and luminous contrasts in the manner of Ribera. This was prior to his great turn-about which brought him to reject the inconsistencies of Impressionism in order to make it "... something more solid and durable, like the art of museums." This silent revolutionary who had learned from the Impressionists to translate the immediate appearances of nature, at a more mature age understood that the luminous vibrations are nothing more than the evanescent and changeable surface of forms, which possess their own life and which the painter can capture through discovering their basic structures. All this had already been understood by the great

masters of the past, from Masaccio and Piero della Francesca to Rembrandt and Goya. But the great achievement of Cézanne was to rediscover it for himself. Cézanne's triumph was a glorious reconquest, which had a determining and decisive influence on all the painting that followed. He himself stated: "I am the primitive of a new art."

PAUL CÉZANNE. *Paul Alexis Reading a Manuscript to Zola.*   *p. 77*

This sketch, which shows some influence of Manet, was painted in the garden of Zola's house in Paris. It remained unfinished because Cézanne, to escape military induction in the War of 1870, went into hiding in his refuge in Provence.

PAUL CÉZANNE.   *Madame Cézanne in Red.*   *p. 78–79*

Painted around 1890, that is, at the same period as his famous *Card Players,* this painting documents Cézanne's determination to substitute a vision of reality obtained through reason rather than through Impressionist sensation. With deeply meditated use of tonal values, the vigorous figure appears as a mass of successive decomposition and recomposition of values, foreshadowing Cubism.

PAUL CÉZANNE.   *The Great Pine Tree.*

This splendid canvas—one of Cézanne's masterpieces—was painted about 1886 in the park of Jas-de-Bouffan, in Provence, which belonged to his father. Just like *L'Estaque* (page 81), this landscape is a magnificent revela-

PAUL CÉZANNE
The Great Pine Tree (1887)
Oil on canvas; 84 x 92 cm.
Belonged first to the poet Joachim Gasquet, Aix-en-Provence, and later to Auguste Pellerin, Paris.
In the Museum since 1951.

80

tion of Cézanne's great conquest. The structure of the subject is transfigured into plastic rhythms. These are attained through an initial decomposition of the elements, which, in the end, re-encounter their compositional unity in an astonishing syncretism of volumes and tonalities.

PAUL CÉZANNE. *L'Estaque.*

This work, yet another masterpiece painted on the outskirts of the small village where Cézanne lived for many years, reveals the master's constructive vision. In the marvelous rising projection of the rocks, the volumes are purposely forced into a compositional scheme which results in an enduring pictorial "reality," rather than the skillfully reproduced exterior appearances of Impressionism. The viewer is able to grasp the weight and the harshness of the stones, as opposed to the bluish strip of sea extending across the distant horizon.

PAUL CÉZANNE
L'Estaque (c. 1892)
Oil on canvas; 73 x 91 cm.
From the collection of
Paul Cassirer, Berlin.
In the Museum since 1953.

81

CLAUDE MONET. *Boating on the Epte.*

The girls in this painting are Blanche and Marthe Hoschedé, daughters from the first marriage of the artist's second wife. Water was one of Monet's favorite themes, from the landscapes of Argenteuil to the famous late waterlilies. But the subject is secondary. What most stands out in this canvas is the intrinsic luminosity of the figures in pink. This is not only derived from the contrast with the background tonalities, but directly from the colors, through a dissolution of volumes into simple chromatic vibrations. It is the starting point of Impressionism, of which Monet was the pioneer, with

CLAUDE MONET
Paris 1840-Giverny 1926
Boating on the Epte (1885–1887)
Oil on canvas; 133 x 145 cm.
Remained in Monet's studio
until his death and
was inherited by his son Michel.
In the Museum since 1953.

his penetrating vision, of which Renoir remarked: "It is nothing but an eye, but what an eye!"

PIERRE-AUGUSTE RENOIR. *The Painter Lecoeur in the Forest of Fontainebleau.*

This youthful study, executed while he was still searching for himself, is accomplished with spatula-like strokes of impasto, ". . . as an exception, because the technique does not serve me well," as he himself wrote. The exuberant colors and the excessive details, which are suggested by the compact entanglement of the forest, reveal an impetuous sensibility, yet to be disciplined by experience.

PIERRE-AUGUSTE RENOIR
Limoges 1841-Cagnes 1919
*The Painter Lecoeur in the
Forest of Fontainebleau*
Oil on canvas; 106 x 77 cm.
Signed and dated at lower right:
"A Renoir 1866".
Belonged to Alfred Cassirer, Berlin.
In the Museum since 1952.

83

PIERRE-AUGUSTE RENOIR.   *Bather with Griffon Dog.*

The parabola of Renoir's development extended from the realist suggestions of Courbet, and the encounters with Corot's evanescences, to his progressive liberties and the conquest of the scintillating, luminous colorism of his last phase.

In this nude—one of Renoir's first—Courbet's influence is still evident. Far from the enchanting "bathers" that he would later paint, this is but an undressed woman. However, the little dog set against the striped garment has the singularity of a detail in a Veronese painting, and the mysterious figure visible among the bushes spiritualizes the realism of the nude.

PIERRE-AUGUSTE RENOIR
Bather with Griffon Dog
Oil on canvas; 184 x 115 cm.
Signed and dated at lower right:
Renoir 1870.
Belonged to A. Pellerin, Paris,
who sold it to Alfred Cassirer, Berlin;
later belonged to a collector in
Basel, who deposited it in the
Basel Kunstmuseum.
Detail above.
In the Museum since 1954.

PIERRE-AUGUSTE RENOIR
Marthe Bérard
Oil on canvas; 128 x 75 cm.
Signed and dated at lower left:
Renoir 79.
Belonged to Paul Bérard and was
inherited by Mme. d'Hybouville,
née Marthe Bérard.
In the Museum since 1951.

PIERRE-AUGUSTE RENOIR.   *Marthe Bérard* and
Pink and Blue.   p. 86–87

Although always agreeable, the portraits of children by Renoir often show
an excessive search for effect through a very skillful technique which de-
pends on too showy colors and minute details.
This portrait of the conventionally well-behaved young lady Marthe Bérard, the daughter of a diplomat, is more restrained, yet somewhat cold in its
Victorian flavor. Nonetheless, the linkage of blacks and blues, whites and
greys is truly masterful. On the other hand, the *Pink and Blue* portrait of
the two girls (on page 87) is prodigiously rich and vaporous. It dates from
the period when Renoir constructed his figures without concern for solidity
of form.

PIERRE-AUGUSTE RENOIR
Pink and Blue
Oil on canvas; 119 x 74 cm.
Signed and dated at lower right.
Renoir 81.
Belonged to M. Cahen d'Anvers,
Paris; then to Gaston Bernheim
de Villers, Paris.
In the Museum since 1951.

PIERRE-AUGUSTE RENOIR
Victorious Venus
Bronze; height 180 cm.
Signed, dated, and numbered:
Renoir 1912 no. 2.
Cast by Alexis Rudier, Paris.
In the Museum since 1951.

PIERRE-AUGUSTE RENOIR
Smiling Lady
Oil on canvas: 42 x 33 cm.
Signed and dated, at right:
Renoir 75.
In the Museum since 1953.

PIERRE-AUGUSTE RENOIR. *Smiling Lady.* *p. 88*

The lady represented is probably Mme. Papillon, the wife of the owner of a restaurant frequented by Renoir, or perhaps the same model who posed for his famous canvas, *La Loge.* The similarity is striking; however, in this work, her expression is sweeter and the painting has an admirable lightness.

PIERRE-AUGUSTE RENOIR. *Victorious Venus.*

Renoir was by no means a great sculptor. Three numbered examples of the voluptuous, unpretentious *Venus,* which lacks the magic of the master's colors, were originally cast. Number 2 belongs to the Museum. Afterwards, there began to mysteriously appear innumerable copies in several European and North American museums. This has happened with sculptures down through the centuries; they have often been reproduced to satisfy the enthusiasts and to encourage the business of the casters, be they authorized or not.

PIERRE-AUGUSTE RENOIR.
Bather Drying Herself (1905)
Oil on canvas; 84 x 65 cm.
Signed at lower right:
Renoir.
Belonged to Bernheim-Jeune, Paris.
In the Museum since 1951.

PIERRE-AUGUSTE RENOIR.   *Bather Drying Herself.*

This is one of the great nudes painted by Renoir, who in his old age was fascinated by the female body. It is said that he sometimes interrupted the painting of a nude in order to paint rose petals as part of an exercise to better capture the velvety luminosity of the feminine skin. The model is Gabrielle, a country girl in the service of Mme. Renoir who often posed for the master. The Museum has another version dated a few years later.

PIERRE-AUGUSTE RENOIR.   *The Little Gleaner.*

This delicious doll is probably a portrait of the daughter of the French poet Catulle Mendès. It is part of Renoir's nacreous phase, which is characterized by exuberant color and glazed surfaces, reminiscent of his youth when he decorated fans and porcelains.

PIERRE-AUGUSTE RENOIR.
The Little Gleaner.
Oil on canvas; 56 x 54 cm.
Signed and dated at lower right:
Renoir 88.
From the collection of
Max Meirowsky, Berlin.
In the Museum since 1952.

PAUL GAUGUIN
Paris 1848-La Dominique,
Marquesas Islands 1903
Poor Fisherman
Oil on canvas;
74 x 66 cm.
Signed and dated, with an
inscription at lower left:
P. Gauguin 96
pauvre pêcheur.
Belonged to Julius
Schmits, who deposited it
in the Kunstmuseum, Basel,
from 1939 to 1953.
In the Museum since 1958.

PAUL GAUGUIN.   *Poor Fisherman.*

Gauguin's painting is a return to basic life of primordial nature. Freed from
the constraints of civilization, isolated on a Polynesian island, Gauguin finally encounters the expressive elements of his refined and profoundly musical sensibilities in the dark bodies of the *"maoris"* and the *"vahinés,"* in
the nude and overpowering beaches, in the tangled vines and brilliant flowers of the tropics. In that luxuriant setting, he discovers linear harmonies,
chromatic surfaces, and rhythms of volumes which bestow on his painting a
grave and mysterious accent.

PAUL GAUGUIN
Self-Portrait.
Oil on canvas; 76 x 64 cm.
Signed and dated, with inscription:
P. Gauguin 1896 Près du Golgotha.
Was in the artist's house in Tahiti;
then sold with all his other possessions
at an auction after his death to Victor
Segalen, a ship's doctor, who sold it to
Ambroise Vollard in Paris.
In the Museum since 1951.

PAUL GAUGUIN. *Self-Portrait.*

Forgotten by all, racked by misery and incurable illnesses, Gauguin painted this self-portrait just a few years before his death. Like Christ near Golgotha, his tragic image bursts forth from the abysses of despair, which are symbolized by the ancestral spirits visible in the penumbra. "My energy of former days," he wrote in one of his last letters to Daniel de Monfreid, "is slowly waning . . . It is written in my life that I am condemned to fall, to rise, and fall again . . . These worries *destroy me . . .*"

93

When in Cologne in 1912, Karl Jaspers was fascinated upon visiting a posthumous exhibition of Van Gogh: "It was," he wrote, "as if a primordial source of existence became visible to me for an instant, as if secret motives of our being revealed themselves to me immediately and completely."

In Van Gogh there was truly an elementary force anxious to show itself, to be recognized, to overflow on to the beings and things that surrounded him, and which perennially met him with repulsion and indifference; "Such a great hearth in his soul, and no one approaches to get warm . . . And men are often unable to do anything, prisoners in I know not what horrible cage. . . ."

This warmth of comprehension which poor Vincent searched for in vain in evangelical love and dedication, he finally found in the communion of artist with nature. "Art," he wrote in the happiness of his discovery, "is man joined with nature: nature, reality . . . but with a significance, a character which the artist brings out, and to which he gives expression, which he redeems, which he liberates, which he illuminates. . . ."

This was the essence of Van Gogh's painting, which he attained through a heroic effort and which ended up destroying his nervous system already attacked by hereditary defects and privations. "Van Gogh's great lesson," according to Charpier and Seghers, "is that of a man chained to an intolerable condition, yet able to overcome its horror by forging his creative instruments in the same fires in which his life is being consumed." In his canvases from 1888 to 1890—those two most rich and tragic years in Arles and Saint-Rémy—one clearly perceives the presence of a creative breath which manages to overcome the barriers of lunacy which periodically gripped him. The immense flatland of Crau, the yellow waves of wheat fields, the flames of cypresses, the golden sunflowers, the mountains that unfold below the clouds, everything shines in the incisiveness of forms, the overpowering intensity of colors, the energetic structure of brushstrokes. All these are images formed in the deep recesses of his spirit and projected onto the canvas with a notable force and an instinctive sense of organization of volumes and spaces.

VINCENT VAN GOGH
Groot Zundert 1853-
Auvers-sur-Oise 1890
Still Life with Flowers
(c. 1886)
Oil on canvas;
54 x 45 cm.
Belonged to Baron
Blauquet de Fuldre, Paris, and
appeared in his sale, 1907.
In the Museum since 1954.

VINCENT VAN GOGH.　*Still Life with Flowers.*

A peaceful and curious work of the painter's first phase while he was still attempting to resolve his quest for luminosity and contorted forms: the cosmic expressionism of his genius.

VINCENT VAN GOGH. *The Arlésienne.*

This is a pictorial transposition of a sketch designed by Gauguin during his dramatic visit with Van Gogh in Arles. It is a portrait of Mme. Ginoux, the café-keeper at the train station. Strongly structured in its constructive lines, the black and white figure gains even greater relief against the reddish wall and the variations of green of the desk and the books.

VINCENT VAN GOGH. *The Schoolboy.* *p. 97*

This wistful characterization is a portrait of one of the younger children of the postman Roulin, the painter's only true friend during his tormented stay in Arles. Already in this portrait, in a somewhat brutal fashion, we see the painter's tendency towards ample surfaces of pure colors. Van Gogh brought this technique to perfection in the portraits of *Camille Roulin* and the *Old Peasant,* which reveal splendid combinations of forms and colors.

VINCENT VAN GOGH. *Walk at Dawn.* p. 98

This is one of the canvases painted by Van Gogh in 1889, during his internment in the Saint-Paul de Mausole Sanatorium in Saint Rémy. It is one of the most moving works by the sick and hallucinating artist. The contorted trees and the frenetic brushstrokes already foreshadow the tempestuous weight of the final landscapes of Auvers-sur-Oise, in particular that ominous *Wheat Field* with the black fluttering of the crows, painted at the onset of his ultimate crisis.

VINCENT VAN GOGH. *Stone Bench.*

This canvas was also painted in the Saint Rémy Sanatorium. It depicts the stone bench on the patio near the fountain which Van Gogh could see through the narrow window of his first-floor room. The intensity of the short directional brushstrokes, which characterizes his work, can also be attributed to the almost obsessive closeness of things observed. "The stroke is not very well divided," he wrote to his brother Théo, "and the tones are often broken, and finally I find myself obliged to resort to impastos à la Monticelli . . . Sometimes I truly believe I am following in his footsteps."

HENRI DE TOULOUSE-LAUTREC. *Comtesse de Toulouse-Lautrec.*

In this delicate painting, which was executed in the tranquil intimacy of a manorial garden, it is surprising not to find the ironic and bitter painter of the *demi-monde* of the cabarets and the *maisoncloses* of Montmartre. It is a tender colloquy with his beloved mother, the only woman who was able to understand the drama of her son tortured by his deformity.

HENRI DE TOULOUSE-LAUTREC. *Two Women.*   *p. 101*

Ever an improvising sketcher, Lautrec was able to establish with rapid and nervous strokes the figures that he surprised as he moved through circuses and theatres backstage; he suggests rather than really constructs the forms. In these impressions, the colors are generally heightened by additional touches to enliven the sketch. It is a technique he used in his posters for the *Moulin Rouge.*

HENRI DE TOULOUSE-LAUTREC
Albi 1864-Château de Malromé 1901
Comtesse de Toulouse-Lautrec (c. 1883)
Essence painting on cardboard;
55 x 46 cm.
Monogram at lower left: *HTL*
Belonged to the painter's cousin, A. M. Séré de Rivières.
In the Museum since 1952.

HENRI DE TOULOUSE-LAUTREC
Two Women
Gouache and pastel on cardboard;
62 x 46 cm.
Signed, dated and dedicated
at lower left:
A Carabin T'H Lautrec 91.
In the Museum since 1952.

HENRI DE TOULOUSE-LAUTREC. *Monsieur Fourcade.*   *p. 102*

The figure of the rich bourgeois stands out with extraordinary naturalness and vivacity of attitude against the background of the barely sketched group of masks. The painting documents a type of the dominating class of the time, delineated with subtle irony.

HENRI DE TOULOUSE-LAUTREC. *Divan.*   *p. 103*

The resigned cynicism of prostitutes perhaps disguises the secret bitterness of these slaves of vice. Lautrec stamped the reflection of his own disgrace in the moral unhappiness of these lost creatures.

HENRI DE TOULOUSE-LAUTREC. *Paul Viaud
as an Admiral.*   *p. 103*

A delightful caricature of an operetta admiral in an imaginary battle against a pirate ship. It is a distant relative of Manet's *Lion Hunter Pertuiset* (p. 63).

HENRI DE TOULOUSE-LAUTREC
Divan (1893)
Gouache and pastel on
cardboard; 66 x 80 cm.
Signed at lower right:
H.T. Lautrec
Hodebert Collection, Paris.
In the Museum since 1958.

HENRI DE TOULOUSE-LAUTREC
Monsieur Fourcade
Gouache and pastel on cardboard
77 x 63 cm.
Signed, dated and dedicated at
top right:
À mon bon ami
Fourcade 89 H.T. Lautrec.
From the collection of
Baron Lafaurie, Paris.
In the Museum since 1952.

HENRI DE TOULOUSE-LAUTREC
Paul Viaud as an Admiral (1901)
Oil on canvas; 139 x 153 cm.
Monogrammed at lower right:
H.T.L.
From the collection of
Comtesse de Toulouse-Lautrec, the
artist's mother, it passed to
Georges Séré de Rivières, Toulouse.
In the Museum since 1951.

103

VALADON, UTRILLO, BONNARD, VUILLARD. *p. 104–105*

These turn-of-century Parisian artists represent tendencies immediately preceding the outbreak of Cubism. Suzanne Valadon left the circus to serve as a model for Renoir, Puvis de Chavannes and Toulouse-Lautrec, then finally to become herself a sketcher and painter. Her son Maurice Utrillo, as a narrator of the Parisian suburbs, balanced himself between primitivism and Post-Impressionism. Pierre Bonnard and Édouard Vuillard belonged to the Nabis group reacting against Impressionism. The Museum owns three works by Vuillard with his flat areas of color juxtaposed with the lucid decorative rhythms that are his characteristic. They are portraits of interesting Parisian personalities, including his mother, who worked as a seamstress to educate him; the Princesse Bibesco; Yvonne Printemps and Sacha Guitry, during their first successes as actresses. By Bonnard, who adds a magical freshness and intensity to his palette as well as chromatic luminescence, the Museum possesses this intimate and scintillating nude.

HENRI MATISSE. *The Plaster Torso* *p. 106*

This subtle painter, always searching for surprises, is a master of lines and a magician of forms with pure, intense, and happy colors. Only a few essential strokes are sufficient for him to recreate a shape, be it a nude or a simple jug.

MAURICE UTRILLO
Paris 1883-Paris 1955
Sacré Coeur de Montmartre and Château des Brouillards
Oil on canvas; 81 x 60 cm.
Signed and dated;
Maurice Utrillo, V, 1934.
Inscribed: *"Sacré Coeur de Montmartre et Château des Brouillards."*
In the Museum since 1947.

SUZANNE VALADON
Bessines 1865-Paris 1938
Nudes
Gouache on paper; 43 x 29 cm.
Signed and dated:
Suzanne Valadon 1919.
In the Museum since 1947.

PIERRE BONNARD
Fontenay-aux-Roses 1867-
Le Cannet 1947
Nude (1930)
Oil on canvas; 80 x 67 cm.
Signed at lower right:
Bonnard.
In the Museum since 1951.

JEAN-ÉDOUARD VUILLARD
Cuiseaux 1868-La Baule 1940
Princesse Bibesco (1912)
Oil on canvas; 112 x 81 cm.
Signed at lower right:
E. Vuillard.
Collection of Princesse Bibesco.
In the Museum since 1958.

ALBERT MARQUET. *Marine Scene.*   *p. 106*

Marquet is a peaceful observer, always offering a balanced reproduction of
nature, in a style halfway between Impressionism and Fauvism. In this canvas, he establishes the limits of his honest and decorative manner of com-
prehending and recording an impression; it is always simple and agreeable.
The canvas is from his Algerian period.

MAURICE DE VLAMINCK. *Marine Scene.*   *p. 107*

Vlaminck's paintings are always interlaced with dense, dark tonalities and
vivid, white brushstrokes, flashing like thunderbolts. Reality is transfigured
in hallucinatory visions of a cold and tempestuous world lost in an unend-
ing winter.

MARIE LAURENCIN. *Composition*   *p. 107*

In every way this is an agreeable composition of delicately suggested objects
and figures—an innocent and rosy "Country Concert" of a fairy tale.

HENRI MATISSE
Le Cateau 1869-Nice 1954
The Plaster Torso (1919)
Oil on canvas; 113 x 87 cm.
Signed at lower right:
Matisse.
In the Museum since 1958.

ALBERT MARQUET.
Bordeaux 1875-Paris 1947
Marine
Oil on canvas; 32 x 40 cm.
Signed at lower left:
marquet.
In the Museum since 1947.

MAURICE DE VLAMINCK
Paris 1876-Paris 1958
Rueil de la Gadelière 1958
Marine
Oil on canvas; 38 x 46 cm.
Signed at lower right:
Vlaminck.
In the Museum since 1947.

MARIE LAURENCIN
Paris 1885-Paris 1956
Composition
Canvas; 51 x 61 cm.
Signed and dated:
Marie Laurencin 1934.
In the Museum since 1948.

107

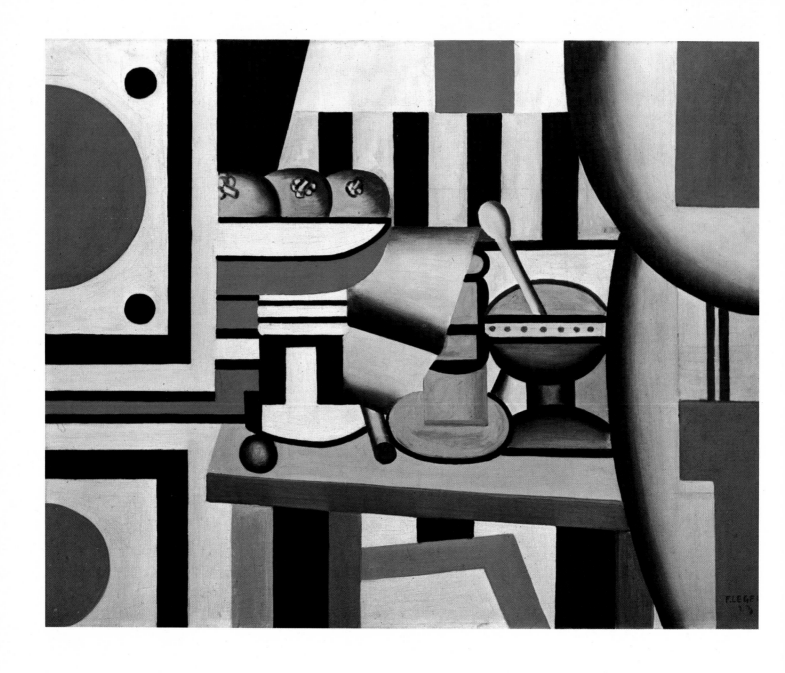

FERNAND LÉGER. *Compote Dish of Pears*

Among the protagonists of contemporary art, Léger oscillates between Cubism and Futurism, while suggesting abstract motives. He is the creator of "pictorial mechanisms," in which even a compote dish or a small pestle acquires the look of a mechanical appliance.

PABLO RUIZ PICASSO. *Toilette.*

Imagination and reality, reflection and improvisation found a thousand surprising and disconcerting languages in Picasso: Impressionism, Romanti-

FERNAND LÉGER
Argentan 1881-Gif-sur-Yvette 1956
Compote Dish of Pears
Oil on canvas; 79 x 98 cm.
Signed and dated at lower right:
F. Léger 23.
Acquired in 1923 in Paris by
the maecenas Olívia Guedes
Penteado, and inherited by her
daughter Carolina da Silva Telles,
who gave it to the Museum in 1947.

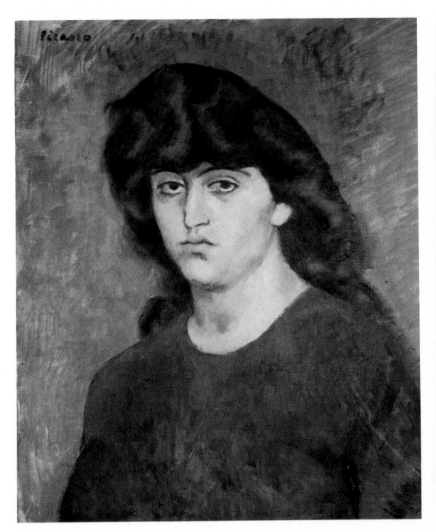

PABLO RUIZ PICASSO
Portrait of a Woman (1904)
Oil on canvas; 65 x 54 cm.
Signed at top left:
Picasso.
From the collection of Princess
Sichnowsky, London, it passed to
Mme. H. Bieber, Lugano, who deposited
it in the National Gallery of Art
Washington, D.C., from 1942 to 1946.
In the Museum since 1947.

PABLO RUIZ PICASSO
Málaga 1881-Mougins 1973
Toilette (1906)
Oil on canvas; 52 x 31 cm.
Signed at lower left:
Picasso.
From the collection of
James P. Warburg, New York.
In the Museum since 1953.

cism in blue, Neo-Classicism in pink, Cubism, exasperated Expressionism, imaginative Surrealism. His motto was always: "I don't search, I find." He was an inexhaustible inventor, in the Latin meaning of the word *inventio;* a find, a discovery in the heart of reality which he intensely observed with that piercing look, and which he would later re-create in unexpected forms, suggested by the sudden revelations he discovered in it. "Abstract art does not exist," he declared, not without malice, "it is necessary to begin from something; but, immediately, one can remove all appearance of reality because the idea of the object leaves its indelible mark."

He was without doubt a genius who renewed and influenced all contemporary art, from painting to sculpture, from decoration to scenography. Perhaps his work brought to a close a great cycle of modern art and leaves a torch to the future which, one day, will be picked up and carried on.

This is a preparatory study, 1906, for the painting in the Albright Art Gallery, Buffalo.

109

PABLO RUIZ PICASSO
The Athlete (1909)
Oil on canvas; 93 x 72 cm.
Signed at lower right:
Picasso.
From the collection of
Ambroise Vollard, Paris.
In the Museum since 1951.

PABLO RUIZ PICASSO.   *Portrait of a Woman*
and *The Athlete.*   *p. 109*

The model for the portrait is Suzanne Bloch, painted by the young Picasso
during his early years in Paris, still under the influence of Impressionism.
In *The Athlete*—one of the first Cubist canvases painted in Horta de Ebro
two years after the famous *Demoiselles d'Avignon*—Picasso sought to ex-
press the strength of the young gymnast's muscles, making the lines of force
stand out from the natural features. At times, his Cubism was more random
than thought out, because he himself said that when he "created" Cubism
he didn't have the slightest intention of doing so, but rather of exteriorizing
what he had intended at the moment.

CHAIM SOUTINE
Smilovitch 1894-Paris 1944
Great Tree (1942)
Oil on canvas; 99 x 75 cm.
Signed at lower right:
C. Soutine.
In the Museum since 1958.

JACQUES LIPCHITZ
Druskieniki 1891-Capri 1973
Pierrot with Mandolin (1925)
Bronze; height 47 cm.
Signed on the base: *Lipchitz.*
From the collection of the maecenas
Olívia Guedes Penteado, inherited by
her daughter Carolina da Silva Telles,
who donated it to the Museum in 1948.

JACQUES LIPCHITZ. *Pierrot with Mandolin.*

As in painting, sculpture of the time looked for new means of expression through the Cubist search. In search of the decomposition of form, the figure curiously evokes the ecstasy of a musician absorbed in strumming his mandolin.

CHAIM SOUTINE. *Great Tree.*

In this landscape painted in the scintillating light of the Mediterranean sun, the magical Expressionist master imprints frenzied torsion on the dramatically simplified tree, glowing in vigorous and brilliant tonalities. Exaltation guides his expression, which is organized on a structural substratum that vibrates in every detail of the whole.

111

112

AMEDEO MODIGLIANI
Renée
Canvas, 61 x 31 cm.
Signed: *Modigliani.*
Inscription:
Renée, Septembre 1917.
Sabouraud Collection, Paris.
In the Museum since 1951.

Upper right
AMEDEO MODIGLIANI
Diego Rivera (1916)
Oil on cardboard; 100 x 79 cm.
In the Museum since 1951.

AMEDEO MODIGLIANI
Livorno 1884-Paris 1920
Léopold Zborowski (1919)
Signed at top right:
Modigliani.
Belonged to Léopold Zborowski, Paris.
In the Museum since 1950.

AMADEO MODIGLIANI. *Léopold Zborowski* and *Renée.*   *p. 112*

The enchanting lyricism of Modigliani's paintings has its origin in the happy meeting of two fundamental sources: the sinuous outlines of the Sienese masters—notably Simone Martini—and the tonal structure of Cézanne. In addition, there is an evident influence of African ritual masks, mysteriously arising from the long totemic necks.

In these two portraits—and even more so in his sketches—the linear arabesque is developed with melodious fluidity, and the attentive looks suggest, rather than reveal, the secret thoughts of the sitters.

AMEDEO MODIGLIANI.   *Diego Rivera.*

The portrait of Diego Rivera is a simple, instantaneous notation of the figure of the Mexican master, singularly different from his other work.

113

MAX ERNST
Brühl, Cologne 1891-Paris 1976
Bryce Canyon Translation.
Oil on canvas; 50 x 39 cm, signed
and dated: *Max Ernst 46.*
In the Museum since 1948.

WOLS, pseudonym of
A. O. SCHULTZE-BATTMANN
Berlin 1913-Paris, 1951
Harmony in
Red-White-Black (1947)
Oil on canvas; 99 x 77 cm.
In the Museum since 1948.

MAX ERNST. *Bryce Canyon Translation.*

Max Ernst's magical world comes together in this canvas. The impact of Surrealist contemplation transforms the steep fractuosities of the canyon into a fantastic Hindu temple swarming with statues under lunar rays.

WOLS. *Harmony in Red-white-black.*

Wols' painting, which has evident links with the work of Klee and other Surrealists, suggests arcane microcosms disclosed by the lens of an electronic microscope.

SPAIN AND PORTUGAL

MESTRE ARTÉS
School of Valencia,
active start of sixteenth century
*The Last Judgment and
Saint Gregory's Mass*
Oil on panel; 200 x 130 cm.
Donated to the Museum by
Daniel Wildenstein in 1967.

MESTRE ARTÉS. *The Last Judgment and Saint Gregory's Mass.*

This is a characteristic work of the Catalan painter, who was a student of Mestre Perea. He was nicknamed Artés after the name of the family who had requested a Judgment for the Cartuxos Chapel in Portacoeli. It presents the traditional concept of the Last Judgment. In the background, a

green cemetery from which the resurrected are carried by angels to Purgatory or by devils to the eternal fire. In contrast to side scenes full of movement, in the center the saint—absorbed in prayer—lifts the host at the hour of consecration.

EL GRECO. *Annunciation.*

This theme was frequently dealt with by El Greco, from his Venetian period and the transition from his Byzantine to his Italian manner, to the overpowering realizations of the Toledo period. It was there, in that atmosphere dominated by Saint Teresa of Avila's mysticism, that El Greco attained the apex of his glowing expressionism of lights and colors. In this work, as in his other masterpieces, the scene is conceived through plastically distinct zones linked by rhythms which resound to each other in a musical fashion. The circular movement created by the attitudes of the Virgin and the archangel is interrupted by the parallel curves of the angel's and the dove's wings between flashes of surreal light, which are reflected in the lively chromatic harmonies of the two figures.

FRANCISCO ZURBARÁN. *Saint Anthony of Padua.*   *p. 117*

Quite different from El Greco's flaming ecstasy, this figure by Zurbarán is characterized by the gloomy conventional mysticism obsessed with mortification, which dominated Spain of the period.

DIEGO VELÁZQUEZ. *Count-Duke of Olivares.*

The history, indeed, the episodes involving this painting reveal how the process of criticism dedicated to attributions can, at times, fall into apparently unmanageable error. When we acquired the canvas in 1948 from Lord Cowdray of London, it was accompanied by a pedigree full of reservations. When it was placed on sale at Sotheby's in London in 1947, it received almost no attention. The interested parties based themselves on several old opinions. A. de Beruete believed that the painting was a copy of the lost original, which might have been destroyed in the 1734 fire in the Alcazar. In the opinion of August L. Mayer, it was an autograph work by Velázquez. J. R. Mélida had published in the Madrid *Revista de Archivos* of 1906, the signed receipts given by the master—today the property of the Metropolitan Museum of New York—for three paintings commissioned by Doña Antonia de Ipeñarrieta: one of Philip IV (Metropolitan Museum of New York), another of the Count-Duke of Olivares (Museum of Art, São Paulo) and the third of Don García Pérez de Araciel, her recently deceased husband, a now-lost work.

The first two canvases went through the following collections: Corral Family of Zaraúz, descendants of the Ipeñarrietas, until the beginning of the nineteenth century; the Duke of Granada; the Count of Real; the Duke of Villahermosa; the Duke of Luna. They were bought in 1912 by Agnew of London, who sold them to Duveen, London, who in turn sold them to Benjamin Altman of New York. The latter offered them to the Metropolitan Museum, which chose only the portrait of Philip IV; the Count-Duke remained in the Museum's store-rooms for some time. Sent back to England, the painting was sold to Lord Cowdray. The latter, after unsuccessfully attempting to sell it at the above-mentioned auction, offered it to our Museum for £ 25,000. When the painting arrived in São Paulo, owing to the fact that the city is in Latin America, Beruete's opinion was accepted as correct. This is so true that in our round of Europe, we were invited to catalogue the work as "School of Velázquez." It was difficult to contradict the museum directors who borrowed the collection, but it was also possible to further clear up doubts. We had to establish the relationship between the master's receipt and the work itself. In the first place, it was necessary to free the painting of the varnish mixed with extract of walnut, the *beverone,* as the Italians call it. This had been used to mask the several badly restored areas, such as the left hand, which were the parts that disturbed the critics, except for Lafuente-Ferrari, who always believed in the autography of the attribution. The cleaning was confided to José Guidol, who did a magnificent job in 1962 in São Paulo. From the first dissolution of the varnish, the splendid painting reappeared, dismissing any doubt that it was the work of Velázquez. It is a foreshadowing of Manet's pursuit of Impressionism, and even more of Degas' feathery, dancing strokes.

FRANCISCO GOYA Y LUCIENTES
Ferdinand VII (1814)
Oil on canvas; 83 x 67 cm.
Initialed on the chair back:
FG.
From the collection of
the Viscounts Valderro, Madrid.
In the Museum since 1947.

FRANCISCO GOYA Y LUCIENTES
Fuentes de Todos 1746-Bordeaux 1828
*Cardinal Luís María de Borbón y
Vallebriga,* detail (c. 1800)
Oil on canvas; 200 x 106 cm.
From the collection of the Prince
Eugenio de Ruspoli, Madrid.
In the Museum since 1951.

FRANCISCO GOYA Y LUCIENTES.   *Ferdinand VII.*

At the dawn of the past century appeared the virile painting of Goya. Realist and expressionist, violent and passionate, caustic and gentle—Goya is unclassifiable. He painted princes and plebians, ladies and *majas,* picturesque scenes and bestial cruelties. With his sharp and penetrating vision he observed and transcribed reality, taking in its most incisive aspects with impious verisimilitude. He placed his figures in space with a sure sense of composition and a refined chromatic sensibility, whether he was painting with exuberant gradations, as in his *Parasol,* or depending on two or three tonalities, as in his *Majas on a Balcony.*

In the *Portrait of Ferdinand VII,* just as in the famous *Family of Charles IV,* he consigned the ambition, smugness and pride of these august royal personages to history.

FRANCISCO GOYA Y LUCIENTES.   *Cardinal Luís María de Borbón y Vallebriga.*

The "Cardinal-Infante," son of the morganatic marriage of the Infante Luís of Borbón and Doña María Teresa Vallebriga, was elevated to Archbishop of Toledo at a very young age. The figure is solidly planted in the sequence of the three red "cones" of his vestments, on which hang the insignia of the honorary orders of Charles III and the Holy Spirit.

FRANCISCO GOYA Y LUCIENTES
Don Juan Antonio Llorente (1813)
Oil on canvas; 189 x 114 cm.
From the Llorente family, it
passed to Durand-Ruel, Paris, who
sold it to Eduard Arnhold, Berlin.
In the Museum since 1954.

121

FRANCISCO GOYA Y LUCIENTES. *Don Juan Antonio Llorente.*

p. 121

The smiling figure of Don Llorente, the last Secretary-General and caustic historian of the Spanish Inquisition, has a captivating naturalness. Like Goya, he was a sympathizer of the French Revolution, and both men went into exile in Bordeaux after the Bourbon restoration.

JOSÉ VITAL MALHOA. *Artist and Model.*

This often-painted theme, in innumerable variations down through the centuries, appears here reinterpreted with grace and masterful tonal vibrations.

JOSÉ VITAL MALHOA
Caldas da Rainha 1854-
Figueira dos Vinhos 1933
Artist and Model
Oil on canvas; 93 x 127 cm.
Signed and dated, lower right:
José Malhoa 1894.
In the Museum since 1967.

FLANDERS, HOLLAND
AND GERMANY

HANS MEMLING. *The Virgin, Saint John and the Holy Women.*

Hans Memling was German by birth, but Flemish by choice. In this panel he brings together the Germanic incisiveness of design with the chromatic brilliance of Rogier van der Weyden, his teacher. This admirable composition is balanced between the verticality of the figures which surround the Virgin like a halo and the melodious horizontal undulation of the hands.

HANS MEMLING.
Seligenstadt (Moguncia)
c. 1433-Bruges 1494
*The Virgin, Saint John and
the Holy Women* (c. 1475)
Oil on wood; 51 x 40 cm.
From the collection of the
Marquis de Rochefort, Paris.
In the Museum since 1954.

HANS HOLBEIN, the YOUNGER. *Henry Howard, Earl of Surrey.*

HANS HOLBEIN
THE YOUNGER
Augsburg, c. 1497
Augsburg 1543
*Henry Howard, Earl
of Surrey* (1541–1543)
Oil on panel; 53 x 42 cm.
Inscription in center:
*HENRY HOWARD ERLE OF SURRY
ANNO AETATIS SUAE 25.*
Belonged to the Duke of
Norfolk, Thomas Howard.
In the Museum since 1958.

Holbein, a friend of Erasmus of Rotterdam, executed this admirable portrait in London, where he lived for the last eleven years of his life, court painter to Henry VIII and a friend of Thomas More and other notables. The final phase of Holbein's painting is distinguished by deep psychological characterization of his sitters, without the slightest emotional involvement of the artist. This portrait represents the eldest son of the third Earl of Norfolk, a cousin of Catherine Howard, fifth wife of Henry VIII. Howard was a contradictory, proud, unpredictable and vain man, but nonetheless a suble poet who was the object of debate and envy. He was beheaded in 1547, having been accused of high treason.

125

HIERONYMUS BOSCH. *Temptation of Saint Anthony,* and details.

This is one of the innumerable allegories of that portentous precursor of Surrealism, who was an inexhaustible creator of demonic beings with a moralistic purpose, or at least entertaining for the less susceptible. In this phantasmagoric spectacle, taking in air, land, water and fire, the figure of the saint almost disappears, submerged in the crowd.

LUCAS CRANACH. *Young Bridegroom.* *p. 128*

This is a portrait of a young bridegroom who, according to German custom, decorated his head with a wreath of carnations. The coat of arms engraved in his ring identifies him as a member of the Rava family of Meissen. This painting is characterized by its sharpness of design, tense line, and sculpturesque form similar to Dürer. This friend of Luther, who was the outstanding impresario of the most prolific atelier of Saxony, seems chastened here, obliged to produce a routine theme. It is but a pause in his series of enigmatic allegories, which waver between symbolism of innocent feminity and ambiguous intimations of lust.

HIERONYMUS BOSCH
Hertogenbosch, c. 1450-
Hertogenbosch 1515
Temptation of Saint Anthony (c. 1500)
Oil on panel, 127 x 101 cm.
From the Convent of Santa Sophia,
near Seville.
Details above.
In the Museum since 1952.

REMBRANDT HARMENSZ VAN RIJN. *Self-Portrait with Incipient Beard.*

Rembrandt painted many self-portraits through the years, from his exuberant and extroverted youth until his solitary and miserable old age. They are living testaments of his existence about which no biography could provide more detail. Always an objective observer of himself, without vanity or self-commiseration, without any other purpose than to capture the essential aspects to be reconstructed on the canvas, Rembrandt left us, each time, an image of his mood, which never succumbed to adversity.

This self-portrait of his youth, in which the painter presents himself in fine garments and adorned with a gold chain, must pre-date his marriage to Saskia, the enchanting woman he lived with for seven anxiety-free and happy years in the luxurious mansion on Judenbreestraat, replete with art objects. The portrait shows short, nervous strokes of yellows, reds, and browns and already reveals the maturity of style and virile firmness of the later self-portraits.

REMBRANDT
HARMENSZ VAN RIJN
Leiden 1606-Amsterdam 1669
Self-Portrait with Incipient Beard
(1634–1636)
Oil on panel; 57 x 44 cm.
Signed at right center:
Rembrandt.
From the collection of
Lord Palmerston, London, and
Charles Sedelmeyer, Paris.
In the Museum since 1949.

LUCAS CRANACH
Kronach 1472-Weimar 1553
Young Bridegroom
Oil on panel; 61 x 43 cm.
Signed with monogram, left center,
with the date of 1539.
From the collection of
Ralph Bernal, London.
In the Museum since 1950.

FRANS HALS
Antwerp 1580-Haarlem 1666
Andries van der Horn (c. 1638)
Oil on panel; 86 x 67 cm.
Inscription at right center:
AETAT SUAE 38 / AN 1638
(the date is not clear;
it may be read 1639).
Maria Pietersdochter Olycan (1635-1640)
Oil on canvas; 86 x 67 cm.
In the Museum since 1951.

ANTHONY VAN DYCK
Antwerp 1599-London 1641
*The Marchesa Lomellini and
her Children* (1621-1622)
In the Cattaneo Palace, Genoa,
until 1906, when it was acquired
by B. B. Lihme, New York.
In the Museum since 1951.

FRANS HALS. *Andries van der Horn* and *Maria Pietersdochter Olycan.*

Hals had an astonishing ability to paint likenesses of an impressive exterior veracity with incredible rapidity. The portrait of Andries van der Horn, is identifiable as a figure in the famous group painting *The Saint Adrian Company of Riflemen,* which is found in the Frans Hals Museum in Haarlem. The portrait of his wife, Marie Pietersdochter Olycan, is believed to have been produced at a later date.

ANTHONY VAN DYCK. *The Marchesa Lomellini and Her Children.*

p. 130

This is one of the canvases painted by Van Dyck during his stay in Genoa, when he unfortunately permitted himself to be influenced by the sentimental excesses of Guido Reni. It is a portrait of an aristocratic lady of the city, the Marchesa Lomellini, with her two children, the younger one of whom is wearing a habit for children destined for an ecclesiastical life.

ENGLAND

JOSHUA REYNOLDS. *The Children of Edward Hollen Cruttenden.*

Reynolds was the official painter of the late eighteenth-century pompous and sophisticated high society of England. Very much in vogue, his skillful and excessively refined painting presents characters fixed in studied atti-

JOSHUA REYNOLDS
Plymptom Earl 1723-London 1792
*The Children of Edward Hollen
Cruttenden* (1759–1763)
Oil on canvas; 179 x 168 cm.
Belonged to Elisabeth Cruttenden,
the oldest daughter shown in the
canvas, and to her husband, Charles
Purvis; later, in the collection of
Marshall Field, New York.
In the Museum since 1952.

THOMAS GAINSBOROUGH
Sudbury 1727-London 1788
Drinkstone Park (c. 1760)
Oil on canvas; 155 x 145 cm.
Belonged to the Grimsby family;
purchased from the last descendant
by Sir Kenneth Clark, London, who
sold it to the Museum in 1951.

tudes against a conventional landscape background. Even the sad story of these three children is transformed by his brush into an affected Arcadian scene in which the children carry flowers in memory of their parents. The children, daughters and son of the Director of the East India Company, were mercifully saved by their Hindu nurse when their parents died in the sacking of Calcutta by the nabob of Bengali.

THOMAS GAINSBOROUGH. *Drinkstone Park.*

The celebrated painter of the *Blue Boy* is represented in the Museum by portraits of Arabelle Bolton and of Francis Rawdon, first Marquis of Hastings and Governor-General of India, as well as by this landscape of a well-known place in Suffolk County during one of the intervals between his obligations as a portraitist. Sensitive to suggestions of reality, at a time in England when there was already an interest in recording impressions, Gainsborough knew how to harmonize an idealized scene of nature with a refined coloristic elegance rich in lyrical content like the poetry of Wordsworth.

133

THOMAS LAWRENCE. *The Fluyder Children.*

The virtuosity of Reynold's successor as royal painter and, consequently, painter of the rich bourgeoisie, brings the banal and artificiality to a climax. It satisfied a society which wanted to show itself off: proper physiognomies, prettified faces, emphases on elegance of ball-room dress and romantic

THOMAS LAWRENCE
Bristol 1769-London 1830
The Fluyder Children (c. 1805)
Oil on canvas; 237 x 145 cm.
The painting remained in the Fluyder
family until it was sold to the
Duke of Marlborough, and then to
Marshall Field, New York.
In the Museum since 1952.

poses, all framed in conventional surroundings. The setting in this painting is the fashionable springs of Bath, denoting calmness and economic prosperity, optimum health or health soon to be restored by the miraculous waters. Here we have the rich gentry of Thackeray's novels.

JOHN CONSTABLE. *Salisbury Cathedral.*

Constable was a precursor of the vigorous and free painting which fore-

shadowed Impressionism. He was the first English painter to take his easel into the countryside in order to capture nature in all its authenticity. This is particularly visible in the studies first done in the outdoors and then redone in the studio, to be shown at the Royal Academy, to satisfy the predominating taste for open landscape. Constable was barely appreciated in England; but at the Parisian Salon of 1824 his work caught the attention of Delacroix and thus exerted a decisive influence on French painting.

JOSEPH MALLORD WILLIAM TURNER. *Caernarvon Castle.*

p. 135

Turner is the greatest interpreter of the English landscape. He was the only painter to transcend objective reality and recreate it in purely pictorial terms. He was a solitary eccentric who untiringly roamed through valleys and mountains sketching rapid impressions which he later reconstructed in his studio. He had an exceptional visual memory and was a delicate and sensitive soul behind a hard exterior. He was capable of expressing with but a few light brushstrokes the evanescent atmosphere of an Alpine lake, or the violence of a storm with a fury of colors. He was the Western painter

GRAHAM SUTHERLAND
London 1903-
*Imaginary Portrait
of Admiral Nelson*
Oil on canvas; 60 x 73 cm.
Inscription on verso:
*HORATIO NELSON an imaginary portrait
based on what may be a life mask in the
National Maritime Museum.
G. S. 1965 June.*
Commissioned by Assis Chateaubriand
in London in 1965 and donated by him
to the Museum in the following year.

WINSTON SPENCER CHURCHILL
Blenheim, Oxfordshire 1874-
London 1965
Blue Room in Trent Park
Oil on cardboard; 50 x 34 cm.
Initialed, at lower left:
WSC.
This was the statesman's first painting
to be offered at auction, in a charity
sale at Christie's, organized by his
wife in 1949. A group of Brazilians,
led by Assis Chateaubriand, went to
London to purchase the work at any price.

Above right
JOE TILSON
London 1928-
Studio I (1962)
Oil on canvas and notched
wood panel; 32 x 32 cm.
In the Museum since 1966.

who, like the Chinese, best understood the evocative value of space, and the first to attempt almost abstract harmonies of pure tonalities.

GRAHAM SUTHERLAND. *Imaginary Portrait of Admiral Nelson.*

Only a painter who had documented the behavior of Londoners during the bombings of World War II could have represented the often-wounded hero of Trafalgar in this way. The admirer of Nelson who had commissioned the painting from Sutherland undoubtedly expected a heroic allegory of the celebrated character, but received instead this freely rendered portrait, which exteriorizes quite well the moral judgment of the artist.

WINSTON SPENCER CHURCHILL. *Blue Room in Trent Park.*

One surprise for visitors to the São Paulo Museum is this small oil by the great "Winnie," who, among his hobbies, was a painter. It is a clear and tranquil—very British—interior, painted with the same honesty of hundreds of painters who continue the English tradition of elegant realism.

JOE TILSON; PATRICK PROCTOR; EDUARDO PAOLOZZI.
Studio I; Me, or a Quiet Dinner; Hidra.

The geometric abstraction by Joe Tilson (above) exemplifies the work of one of the most active and versatile artists of the London School, which is also represented in the São Paulo Museum by works of Patrick Proctor and Eduardo Paolozzi, reproduced on the following page.

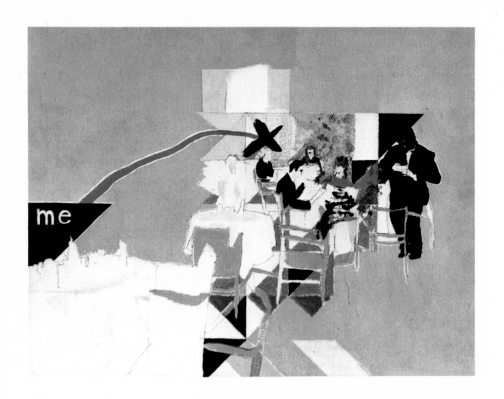

PATRICK PROCTOR
Me, or a Quiet Dinner (1965)
Oil on canvas; 41 x 54 cm.
In the Museum since 1966.

EDUARDO PAOLOZZI
Edinburgh 1924-
Hidra
Chromed metal; 46 x 39 x 9 cm.
In the Museum since 1966.

BRAZIL

The São Paulo Museum does not possess a very extensive collection of Brazilian paintings and sculptures. Both the Sacred Art Museum and the State Museum in São Paulo having been dedicated to the preservation of Brazilian art, we have concentrated our collecting efforts on foreign artists. Nonetheless, some emphasis has been placed on Brasiliana. We have brought together several works which are significant for diverse aspects of our national history—from ethnography to sociology. They are useful in the organization of temporary exhibitions, the centerpiece of the Museum's activities. In future years, the Museum will develop its collection of Brazilian baroque art and complete those of the nineteenth and twentieth century. Although there are many studies available on Brazilian art, its five centuries of existence have yet to be well defined. Occasionally it is relegated to being a backward follower of Portuguese art, while at other times—on the contrary—it is given more importance than it merits. Brazilian art does indeed deserve consideration—naturally within its own limitations—for the originality with which it elaborated and, one might say, nationalized the moods brought from Europe in an attempt to construct a tropical civilization in the Western Hemisphere.

The earliest examples of this are the works of Frans Post, who is considered the first painter to reproduce the landscape of northern Brazil, and the most recent are by the outstanding Brazilian artists of this century. It is a limited panorama, but one which gives an idea of what has happened in Brazil. In the seventeenth century, exoticism became the fashion in Europe owing to the intensification of commerce with the Far East, Africa, and America, all symbolically synthesized in the word "Indies." An example of this is the group of Gobelins tapestries entitled *Series of the Indies*. Except for the inclusion of elephants, it presents facts of Brazilian nature. The origin of the tapestries is linked to the role of the Dutch in the development of the Northeast. During the first half of the seventeenth century, a colony of the Dutch West India Company was implanted there, headed by Prince Maurice of Nassau. On his estate, Mauritshuis, near Recife, he had a miniature court, with architects, painters, and distinguished researchers in different fields who produced works of scientific interest. Nassau had three painters in his service: Frans Post, Albert Eckhout and Zacharias Wagener, the first two Dutch, and the last German. They were charged with sketching every aspect of the New World, particularly its riches. Thus, in addition to the preparation of topographic maps and other documents useful in case of war, these artists dedicated themselves to the depiction of native life and landscapes in pathetically optimistic scenes. According to Montaigne, it was a world ". . . so new and so childlike that it still had to be taught its ABCs." The "Indies" tapestries are based on a series of forty-two canvases by Frans Post and Albert Eckhout, which were part of a gift from Maurice of Nassau to Louis XIV in 1679; also included were sketches, artifacts, and even zoological specimens. Nassau suggested that, being based on such materials, the King should be able ". . . to furnish a large room or gallery with tapestries which would represent things of great rarity, not found anywhere

GOBELINS TAPESTRY
Hunter at Rest (1692–1700)
Tapestry; 323 x 214 cm.
Acquired from the Countess of Abingdon, London.
In the Museum since 1950.

else in the world." This is the origin of the considerable Brazilian collection in the Louvre. The tapestries, each one made up of eight pieces, were executed in the Gobelins manufactory. There were three series, dating from 1687 to 1730. From the third series the Museum possesses five pieces—*The Elephant,* the *Hunter at Rest,* the *Tapir and the Tiger,* and the *Oxen*—woven between 1692–1700.

Frans Post is one of the earliest illustrators of the exotic genre. He is exceptionally important for Brazil because he was the first European artist to document the tropical landscape and lifestyle. Although he returned to his homeland in 1644, he continued to paint scenes of Brazil throughout his life. These almost always include studies of curious animals, such as armadillos, snakes, and anteaters, which were valued more as documents rather than as works of art. The exotic sketch has as its basis a painting that harmonizes illustrative objectivity with a sensitive contemplation of its color structure.

We saw that in the first decade of the nineteenth century, when the royal family moved from Portugal to Rio de Janeiro, Brazil was confronted with

HENRY CHAMBERLAIN
England 1796-Bermuda 1844
Rigging Point in Niteroi
Oil on canvas; 75 x 152 cm.
Acquired in London in 1950.

a number of aesthetic problems in city planning, architecture, theatre, painting, sculpture, and crafts. To improve this situation, in which Rococo styles and moods were still dominant, King John VI invited a mission of French artists to organize an Academy. This resulted in the officialization of a Neo-Classicism which had already been weakened in Europe by the wave of Romanticism and became eclectic in manner. Rio de Janeiro was no longer the capital of a colony but rather of a Kingdom and later on of an Empire, and thus attracted a considerable number of European artists in search of work and adventure. In the first half of the nineteenth century, the capital became a seedbed of painters, sketchers, lithographers, and photographers, some of whom had arrived along with scientific expeditions or diplomatic missions.

FRANS JANSZ POST. *Pernambuco landscape with Mansion,* detail, and *Paulo Afonso Waterfall.* *p. 142*

Although painted in Holland after Frans Post's return to his homeland, these landscapes lost nothing of the intense luminosity and the episodic immediacy which the artist developed during his seven-year stay in Pernambuco. These nostalgic recollections of Northeastern rocks, water, and sky, of fields populated by heavily overdressed whites and semi-nude blacks possess an innocent and captivating grace.

HENRY CHAMBERLAIN. *Rigging Point in Niterói.*

This colorful and lively landscape of Niterói, full of small figures in the style of the period, was painted by Chamberlain, an official of the British

143

JEAN-BAPTISTE DEBRET
Paris 1798-Paris 1848
Slave Hunter
Oil on canvas; 80 x 112 cm.
In the Museum since 1951.

Navy, during a visit of His Majesty's fleet to the waters of the Bay of Guanabara. An amateur painter like many of his compatriots, Chamberlain later collected his impressions of the Bay in an evocative album of watercolors, *Picturesque Views of Rio de Janeiro and its Environs,* which was much sought after by the enthusiasts of exotic scenes.

JEAN-BAPTISTE DEBRET. *Slave Hunter.*

The author of the famous *Voyage Pittoresque et historique au Brésil* was the most faithful illustrator of the life and customs of Rio de Janeiro. He arrived in 1816, at the request of King John VI with the Le Breton mission, to participate in the creation of a "Royal Academy of Sciences, Arts, and Professions." During fifteen years, in his innumerable watercolors and lithographs, he illustrated all aspects of interior and exterior life in the city of Rio de Janeiro with an almost photographic incisiveness and surprising expressive faithfulness. The minute descriptions of objects, utensils, foods and popular dress by themselves constitute a precious ethnographic documentation of the period.

His first paintings of Indians, however, were not as successful, but merely imaginative and without any relationship to indigenous reality. In this *Slave Hunter,* there are imaginary fair-skinned Indians who parade in a Neo-Classic landscape more reminiscent of Poussin or David than the authentic Brazilian forest.

MARIA GRAHAM. *View of the Bay of Guanabara.*   *p. 145*

The author of a *Journal of a Voyage to Brazil,* Maria Graham was an intimate of Dom Pedro I's court and a governess of the Imperial princesses.

MARIA GRAHAM
Papcastle 1785-London 1842
View of the Bay of Guanabara, detail
Oil on canvas; 18.5 x 357 cm.
In the Museum since 1950.

NICOLAS-ANTOINE TAUNAY
Paris 1755-Paris 1830
Rodrigo de Freitas Lagoon
Oil on panel; oval, 8 x 10 cm.
In the Museum since 1951.

Aside from a collection of watercolors which illustrate scenes and customs of the period, she painted several landscapes of Rio de Janeiro in oil, such as this rather simple work of topographical value.

NICOLAS-ANTOINE TAUNAY. *Rodrigo de Freitas Lagoon.*

Nicolas Taunay, along with Debret and Grandjean de Montigny, was one of the most important participants in the French Artistic Mission of 1816; he was also the father of the future Viscount of Taunay. In Rio, from 1816 to 1821, he painted and engraved urban and suburban scenes, historical scenes and family portraits. His palette is notable, as in this oval composition with its effects of chiaroscuro.

LUÍS CARLOS PEIXOTO.   *The Revolt of September 6, 1893.*

The paintings of amateurs, namely of painters usually called "primitives," has had a great development in Brazil ever since the discovery of the country. The colonizer had to provide all the implements for living, and the artistic production reflects his spirit of spontaneous improvisation and communication. The tradition of "naïve painting" continued for a long period. This amateur portrayed the episode of the naval revolt of 1893 with a surprising sense of observation and a certain humor. This is evident in the detail of the man in white who observes the event with visible emotion and the little old man dressed in black who turns his back, angered by the disorderly rebels.

PEDRO AMÉRICO DE FIGUEIREDO E MELO.   *Peace and Concord.*

p. 147

There are two ways of interpreting history in Brazilian painting of the nineteenth century: the courtly manner of the grandiloquent compositions of the official artists, and the simple manner of artists and illustrators without formal training. The first wave the patriotic flag with a confused blending of rhetoric; the latter group, not knowing where to place a flight of angels

LUÍS CARLOS PEIXOTO
Active end of nineteenth century
The Revolt of September 6, 1893
Oil on canvas; 66 x 105 cm.
Signed: *Peixoto.*
In the Museum since 1947.

or a row of columns, limited themselves to a realistic narration of events. Since both are documentary products of our national history, the Museum was interested in collecting works of each of these tendencies, such as that of Luís Carlos Peixoto on the previous page, and Pedro Américo, a student of Ingres and Horace Vernet, who was also a writer, scientist and politician. This canvas praises the Golden Rule, through which Princess Isabel abolished slavery in Brazil.

NICOLA ANTONIO FACCHINETTI. *Bay of Ilha Grande.* p. 148

There were many landscape artists in Brazil in the nineteenth century. Facchinetti, who came from Italy, opened a Florentine-style atelier in Rio, where he executed upon request panoramas of Guanabara and views of plantations. Other artists had studios which specialized in copies of classical works, portraits, or religious paintings.

BENEDITO CALIXTO DE JESUS. *Market at the Dock, Santos, 1885.* p. 148

Calixto was the artisan painter who accepted any kind of commission: decorating churches or theatres, portraits from sittings or based on photographs, historic canvases, documentary landscapes, or souvenirs for tourists. He had attended courses and free academies in Paris, but his vocation was that

PEDRO AMÉRICO DE
FIGUEIREDO E MELO
Areias 1843-Florence 1905
Peace and Concord
Oil on canvas; 42 x 60 cm.
Signed and dated at lower right:
P. Américo 1895.
In the Museum since 1947.

NICOLA ANTONIO FACCHINETTI
Treviso 1824-Rio de Janeiro 1900
Bay of Ilha Grande
Oil on canvas; 28 x 56 cm.
Signed and dated, at lower right:
N. Facchinetti 1869.
In the Museum since 1947.

BENEDITO CALIXTO DE JESUS
Itanhaém 1853-São Paulo 1927
Market at the Dock, Santos, 1885.
Oil on canvas, 30 x 50 cm.
Signed at lower right.
B. Calixto.
Inscription and date,
at lower left:
Caes do Mercado em 1885 Santos.
In the Museum since 1947.

of a provincial factotum. When he painted for himself, however, he was a proficient landscapist with spontaneous ingenuity. He was a "primitive" painter, a category still quite common in today's Brazil.

VÍTOR MEIRELES DE LIMA. *Moema.* *p. 149*

Vítor Meireles is a painter of Brazilian history. He became a popular idol owing to his grand compositions celebrating contemporary or previous national battles. His paintings contain meticulously studied details, garnered from a collection of documents and a wardrobe of uniforms. He managed to give his scenes a certain movement which accentuated the epic quality without, however, dramatizing the severity of the conflicts. With the passage of time, his works take on the character of a ballet. Meireles also dedicated himself to the iconography of works by authors who sought to revive truly indigenous romanticism, without resorting to European models. One example of this tendency is the legend of Moema, evoked in the poem *Caramuru* by Santa Rita Durão. When Diogo Álvares embarked for France with his wife Paraguaçu, five Indian maidens threw themselves, in vain, into the sea to reach the boat; one of them, Moema, managed to seize the rudder of the

ship but was unable to resist the strength of the currents. She was discovered dead on the beach. Meireles also distinguished himself in 1885 with a circular panorama of the Bay of Guanabara measuring 1,667 square meters, which was done in conjunction with the Belgian painter Henri Langerock. The panorama was exhibited in Brussels in 1888. It was mounted on a revolving cylinder and had the patriotic aim of encouraging emigration to Brazil.

JOSÉ FERRAZ DE ALMEIDA JÚNIOR. *Young Girl.*

The painter of this girl in a romantic pose was one of the artists chosen for study in Europe by the Emperor Dom Pedro II, who was a humanist, a maecenas, and a firm believer in the need to promote art and culture. In Paris, although Almeida Júnior chose Alexandre Cabanel as his teacher, he was not notably influenced by him. Upon his return to São Paulo, he became a well-known artist and dedicated himself in particular to scenes of farmers and prospectors.

BELMIRO DE ALMEIDA. *Boys Playing Games.* p. 150

In the second half of the last century, the Academy of Rio de Janeiro produced a large number of painters who can generically be included in Post-Impressionism. They were caught up in ideas and attitudes somewhere between realism and idealism, which led them to professional rather than artistic successes. The most diligent members were awarded study grants by the Academy and they generally used them in Paris, where they sought training from the teachers of the École des Beaux-Arts. Belmiro was one of the few painters to know about the works of the *Nouvelle Peinture,* in particular that of Cézanne and Seurat. His work is not well defined, but it is without doubt most notable, owing to his role in the renewal of Brazilian painting.

JOÃO BATISTA DA COSTA. *The Prisoner.* p. 151

Batista da Costa, who was a student, teacher and Director of Rio de Janeiro's Academia de Belas-Artes, is a painter who did not want to touch new, unaccepted ground. However, he still managed from time to time to break the bonds of his training and paint rural scenes with candor and emotion.

ARTUR TIMÓTEO DA COSTA. *Lady in Green.* p. 151

When the ability to invent one's own mood and style of pictorial production is absent, then routine themes contribute to its lack of spirit and authority. This is true of the nineteenth century. It is indeed curious how some Brazilian artists living in a world of exceptional natural beauty and musicality, a

BELMIRO DE ALMEIDA
Serro 1858-Paris 1935
Boys Playing Games.
Oil on canvas; 30 x 40 cm.
Signed at lower right:
Belmiro.
In the Museum since 1947.

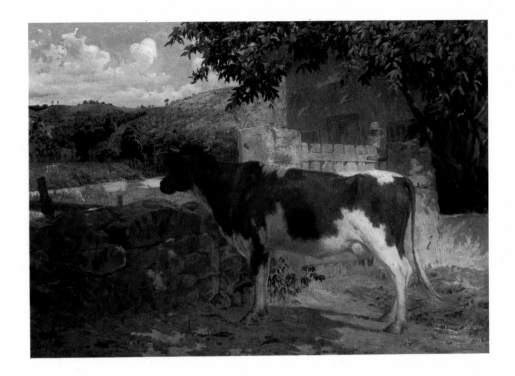

JOÃO BATISTA DA COSTA
Itaguaí 1865-Rio de Janeiro 1926
The Prisoner
Oil on canvas; 66 x 92 cm.
Signed and dated at lower left:
J. Baptista 1905.
In the Museum since 1947.

racial melting pot with vast numbers of myths and so many other offerings of the tropics, did not dedicate themselves to the presentation of their own atmosphere, but turned instead to the repertoire of the European Academy. Timóteo is an example of this tendency.

ARTUR TIMÓTEO DA COSTA
Rio de Janeiro 1882-
Rio de Janeiro 1923
Lady in Green
Oil on canvas; 50 x 61 cm.
Signed and dated at lower right:
Paris 908 Art. Timotheo.
From the collection of Frederico Barata,
Rio de Janeiro, who donated it to
the Museum in 1947.

151

CASTAGNETO and VISCONTI.

Giovanni Battista Castagneto and Eliseu Visconti were two painters, sons of Italian immigrants, who made a contribution to Brazilian art. Castagneto came to Brazil when he was thirteen. Unable to tolerate the classes at the Academy, he transformed a ship into his studio, and sailed about the Bay of Guanabara, painting an infinite number of impressions of it. Owing to their sharp clarity, they were much sought after by visiting foreigners.

Eliseu Visconti also arrived in Brazil as a child and after having finished classes at Rio's Academy of Fine Arts, he went off to Paris. There he discovered the most recent attitudes towards academic Romanticism and Pointillism. His fine portraits attracted attention at the late-century Parisian Salons. Upon returning to Brazil, he dedicated himself to great decorative panels, such as the scenery for Rio's Municipal Theatre. He also contributed graphics and ceramics.

LASAR SEGALL. *Room with Poor Family.*   *p. 154*

A companion of Chagall, born in Vilna, Lasar Segall studied at the Berlin and Dresden Academies in his youth and participated in German Expressionism. In 1913, in São Paulo and Campinas, he was the first vanguard painter to exhibit works which were then beyond the comprehension of the esthetically limited public in the two cities. After spending ten years in Europe, he returned to Brazil without his aggressive spirit. He painted social themes, such as the Mangue red-light district. During the war years, his humanitarian and religious vocation made him consider the war tragedies, the concentration camps, and the pogroms. He had a solitary existence in Brazil, with a few student followers who learned little from his instruction; he was never invited to represent the country at Brazilian sections of the Venice Biennials. Nonetheless, the twenty-ninth exhibition of that institution posthumously dedicated a retrospective to him which was quite a revelation

GIOVANNI BATTISTA CASTAGNETO
Genoa 1862-Rio de Janeiro 1900
Naval Review, detail
Oil on canvas; 74 x 150 cm.
Signed and dated at lower right: .
B. Castagneto 1887.
In the Museum since 1949.

ELISEU VISCONTI
Salerno 1867-Rio de Janeiro 1944
Nude
Oil on canvas; 165 x 89 cm.
Initialed at lower right: *E.V.*
Dated, at top left: *95.*
In the Museum since 1966.

153

for the European public, in particular the works dating from his expressionist period.

The *Room with Poor Family* belongs to that period and is characterized by the search for desolate psychological attitudes. These are attained above all through the exteriorization of intimate states of suffering and through a dramatic simplification of lines and essential tonalities.

EMILIANO DI CAVALCANTI. *Five Girls from Guaratinguetá.*

p. 155

This 1930 canvas already reveals, although in a still youthfully impulsive manner, the chromatic and plastic exuberance of this patriarch of Brazilian art. During his frequent stays in Paris, he passed through phases of appreciation of Grosz, Lhote, and Picasso. He finally dedicated himself to interpreting with a subtle refined liveliness, the figures and landscapes of life in

154

LASAR SEGALL
Vilna 1891-São Paulo 1957
Room with Poor Family
Oil on canvas; 85 x 40 cm.
Signed and dated at lower right:
Segall 20.
In the Museum since 1950.

Rio de Janeiro. His leit-motiv is the sumptuous bodies of nude or partially-dressed mulatto women among multicolor birds and flowers.

FLÁVIO REZENDE DE CARVALHO. *Sleeping Nude.* *p. 156*

Carvalho was an artist of varied interests and a typical representative of the Brazilian vanguard, owing to his polemical spirit and participation in life. He studied engineering and architecture in London. Upon returning to Brazil, he became involved with various initiatives in the fields of agriculture and industry; he designed buildings inspired by *De Stijl* rationalism; he did Cubist sculptures; he wrote plays with philosophical intent; he was involved in sociological experiments which almost caused his public lynching. But, most specifically, he dedicated himself to painting and sketching—the latter in an incisive and disquieting manner.

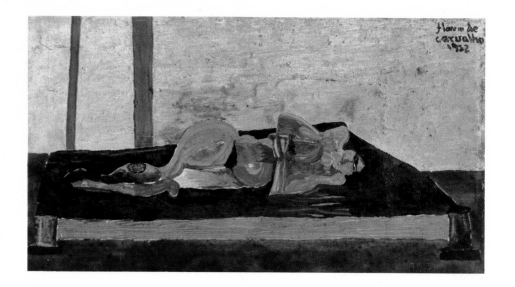

FLÁVIO REZENDE DE CARVALHO
Amparo da Barra Mansa 1899-
Valinhos 1973
Sleeping Nude
Oil on canvas; 32 x 56 cm.
Signed and dated at top right:
flavio de carvalho 1932.
Donated to the Museum by
the artist in 1948.

ANITA MALFATTI. *Russian Student.*

Instead of travelling to Paris, as did most Brazilian artists, Anita Malfatti went off to Berlin. She was a student of Lovis Corinth and became interested in Expressionism. In 1917, she returned to São Paulo and was violently criticized at her first exhibition. The most popular writer and journalist of the time labelled her painting as paranoid, which is a reflection of a society completely unprepared to consider art. In 1948, long after her adventures in vanguard art had been forgotten, the Museum organized a retrospective exhibition to reevaluate the painter.

CÂNDIDO PORTINARI
Brodósqui 1903-
Rio de Janeiro 1962
Refugees from Drought-stricken Region
Oil on canvas; 190 x 180 cm.
Signed and dated at lower right:
Portinari 944.
In the Museum since 1948.

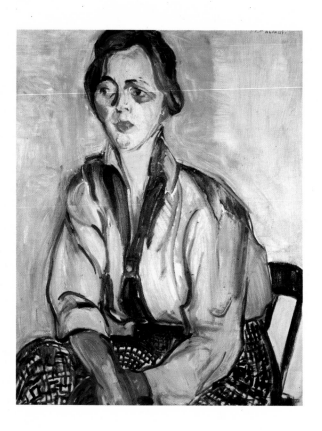

ANITA MALFATTI
São Paulo 1896-São Paulo 1964
Russian Student (1917)
Oil on canvas; 78 x 62 cm.
Signed at top right:
A. Malfatti.
Donated to the Museum by
the artist in 1949.

CÂNDIDO PORTINARI. *Refugees from Drought-stricken Region*

The Museum has an ample collection of the works of Portinari, who is the Brazilian painter best known abroad owing to his murals in the Library of Congress in Washington and in the Headquarters of the United Nations in New York.

This painting is one of a series of three which touch on the tragedy of the poverty-stricken Northeasterners, who are periodically hit by droughts. The essence of these paintings is a rude, provocative expressionism, which aims at exteriorizing the suffering by exaggerating attitudes and gestures, sometimes approaching caricature. The few basic tonalities—whites, greys, and browns—have the sole aim of strengthening the structural context, which is here and there enlivened by a few warmer touches which are merely decorative in value.

158

ERNESTO DE FIORI
Rome 1884-São Paulo 1945
The Brazilian
Plaster; height 100cm.
Initialed and dated on the base:
E. de F. 38.
Donated by the artist's brother,
Mário de Fiori, in 1947.

DE FIORI and ZAMOISKY.

Sculpture was never a popular art in Brazil, with the exception of some outstanding seventeenth-century religious artists—Friar Agostinho da Piedade, Friar Agostinho de Jesus and, of course, Aleijadinho, who left a powerful series of architectural and sculptural works in the state of Minas Gerais. In the nineteenth and twentieth centuries there have been several good sculptors, but the Museum does not possess any of their works. Instead, it has pieces by two foreign sculptors who worked here: Ernesto de Fiori and August Zamoisky.

The Brazilian is one of the thirteen plaster sculptures that the Museum received as a donation from the family of the Italian sculptor Ernesto de

AUGUST ZAMOISKY
Jablon, Poland 1893-
St.-Clair de Rivière 1969
Portrait of Assis Chateaubriand (1952)
Bronze; height 156 cm.
In the Museum since 1968.

Fiori, a naturalized German who took refuge in São Paulo when Hitler began to persecute the so-called "degenerate art."

After a short span of activity as a painter, which he took up once again towards the end of his life, de Fiori dedicated himself to sculpture. He was attracted by the simple beauty of the human body, without any allegorical or social allusions. But this realism was just a point of departure for a sculpture which gradually attained profound, penetrating psychological depths, especially in portraits.

The presence of the cosmopolitan Pole Zamoisky brought attention to possibilities in the field of sculpture. Zamoisky possessed an excellent humanistic background. He had studied in Munich and, after World War I, he participated in the organization of the Cubist tendency group in Warsaw. He received the Grand Prize for Sculpture at the Parisian International Exposition of 1937. In 1940, he arrived in Brazil. He returned to Europe in 1955, working on large sculptures in an atelier on the outskirts of Toulouse.

CONTEMPORARIES

The Museum, as can be observed in the chapters dedicated to the different schools, collects works of contemporary artists, especially Brazilians—which are the easiest to obtain. It is interested in widely debated works of varied tendencies; it has organized "Happenings," and thus has extended itself in an open manner to artists. Obeying the Museum's criterion of alternating exhibitions, paintings, sculptures, and other objects are presented with didactically adequate information. Works in progress also receive complete support in the Museum. The Museum has works by the most active modern artists, including: Wesley Duke Lee, Bernardo Cid, Caciporé Torres, Nelson Leirner, Gastão Manoel Henrique, Maria Helena Chartuni, Fernando Odriozola, Sheila Brannigan, Tomie Ohtake, Carlos Blank, Umberto Espindola, Maurício Salgueiro and others.

THE BUILDING

The Museum building was planned by the architect Lina Bo Bardi in 1957 and was inaugurated in 1968; thus, its construction took ten years. The same architect had been responsible for the first home of the Museum, which was opened to the public in 1947, as well as for mounting the temporary exhibitions which have always been one of the institution's fundamental activities.

Located on Avenida Paulista, where, at the beginning of the century, the so-called coffee barons built their mansions, the Museum stands where Avenida Paulista crosses Avenida Nove de Julho, a traditional meeting place romantically called the *Trianon*. At that particular spot there was a modest belvedere with a good view of the city, which still awaited its first skyscrapers. Beneath the belvedere there was a meeting hall for political or literary meetings, although balls and receptions were also quite frequently held there. The land had been donated to the City with the condition that the belvedere be preserved, a condition imposed on the architect. Accordingly, she designed an open space at the level of Avenida Paulista which covers the hall constructed below ground—a replacement for the meeting hall, which was yet another request of the municipal authorities.

After these initial problems had been satisfactorily resolved, the building was reviewed as being an important element of urban planning, capable *a priori* of gaining the public's acceptance. Resorting to the concept of "spectacular," which characterizes a large part of Brazilian architecture, and keeping in mind that the unusual is more common than the usual, a rational, functional structure in a simple, regular form was chosen.

The plot of land has a slope of thirteen meters and is surrounded by streets. The architect planned a completely open structure, re-creating the artificial plaza and belvedere and dividing the building into two parts: the lower, below the ground level of Avenida Paulista, and the upper. The Auditorium, seating 100 people, and the Theatre, seating 500 people, are located on the lower level and are used for classes, congresses, conferences, concerts, fashion shows, and theatrical and experimental performances. The rest of the lower level area includes a hall for large exhibitions and meetings, as well as storerooms, photographic laboratories and studios, and other services and installations. The large hall is entered through two 14-meter-long overhanging staircases embedded in a footing. The Belvedere, which now became a new public plaza, is paved with parallelepiped granite slabs and surrounded by gardens and pools with aquatic plants; it is used for expositions, shows, and outdoor concerts.

A staircase and a steel elevator with a capacity of 36 persons—an open structure enclosed in tempered glass—link the three floors. The upper part of the building has two floors and the roof has a horizontal area of 2,200 square meters with 5-meter lateral overhangs; both structures are supported on four pillars measuring 4 by 2.5 meters. Each of these pillars carries a vertical load of 2,300 tons, and has a bending strength of 5,000 tons per sq. meter through four large prestressed beams. Two of these beams support the roof, which has a total span of 74 meters; each one supports a weight equal to a 15-meter width of cover-slab. They are simply supported beams, with a liberty of movement in the direction of the axis of the beam because they are firmly set in a pendulum of 6.7 meters in height. This liberty of movement is essential owing to the effects of temperature and shrinkage. These pre-cast concrete beams have 62 cables of 36 5mm. strands. The beams which support the two floors below are also pre-cast and can resist a maximum bending movement of 20,000 tons per square meter along their 4-meter span. Because these beams must be free for horizontal displacement (otherwise the stress would be too great), it was decided to use hydraulic support, specifically support on a bag of oil confined in neoprene. The floor supported by the two beams measures 70 x 30 meters with a coverslab caisson in reinforced concrete with a height of 50 meters. The height of the upper floor, supported on the beams, includes a 4 centimeter coverslab supported on several ribs.

These calculations for the structure were made by consulting engineers, under the direction of the engineer José Carlos de Figueiredo Ferraz, who used his own patent for prestressed concrete. The second floor houses the Museum proper. During the day it is lighted with sunlight, and at night with iodine vapor lamps which are placed at the sides so as to reflect the white-washed ceiling. All traditional finishing touches were completely eliminated from the building; even the reenforced concrete surfaces received no special treatment. All the functional installations are in evidence. The windows on the two floors are made of plate glass measuring 6 meters in height—the largest ever made in Latin America. The floor is of an industrial-type black rubber. The building's architecture was generally well accepted, although within museological circles there were debates about the novelty of the architect's proposals, and about the plans for the exhibition of paintings.

Taking into account that a painting is born in a free space—that is, on an easel—its original state can best be evoked when it is exhibited on tempered plate glass fixed on a concrete base, rather than against an opaque wall. We concluded that it would be arbitrary to hang a painting which the artist did for a specific ambience, on a wall of one color or another. For example, the four portraits of the daughters of Louis XV by Nattier (which are part of the Museum's collection) were destined for the Dauphin's study in the Palace of Versailles. It would be wrong to hang them on a wall; we preferred to exhibit them freely on an easel. Nonetheless, the paintings in our Museum are not loosely exhibited without regard to their historical context. Behind each canvas, on the wall, there are plaques with informative, well-thought out explanations, illustrated with reproductions, engravings, maps, graphics, and documents which can help the visitor to understand the work in question. Initially, this system caused much surprise and was criticized by conservatives; however, the exact opposite occurred with the younger generation—the fifteen- to thirty-year-olds, who readily accepted and liked this innovation.

The first floor is made up of a hall which gives access to the books and magazine sales shop and to the temporary exhibitions hall, measuring 630 square meters. The hall is flanked by two corridors through which one can reach the technical work areas and the administrative offices (Director's office, administration, conservation, exhibition planning, collections, audio-visual productions, Institute for Art History, library, photograph collection, record collection, courses, and film and music departments. The walls of the offices along the corridors are of glass, which further emphasizes the sense of space and the comfort of the atmosphere. The rooms are divided by movable walls.

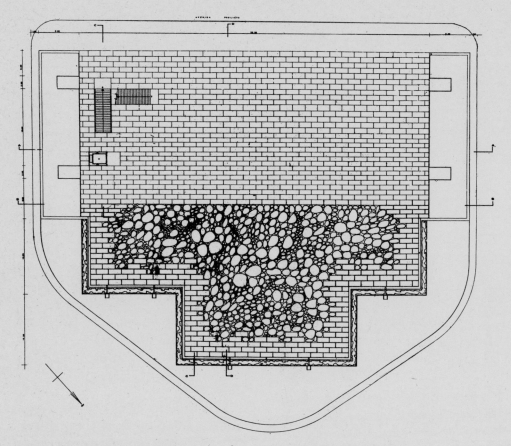

São Paulo Museum of Art: Avenida Paulista level (code 00). The great Belvedere is completely free of structures. The four pillars which support the upper block rise up out of two reflecting pools which receive the falling rain from the roof.

Basement floor below the street level of Avenida Paulista (code -4.50) with the Convention Hall, the small and large auditoriums and other services.

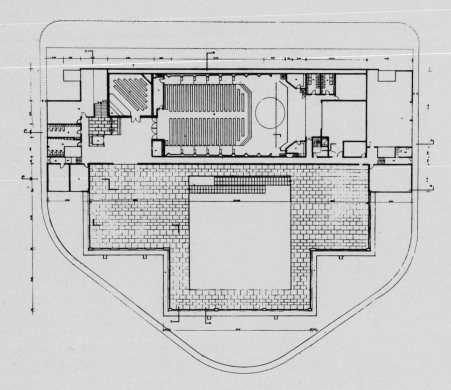

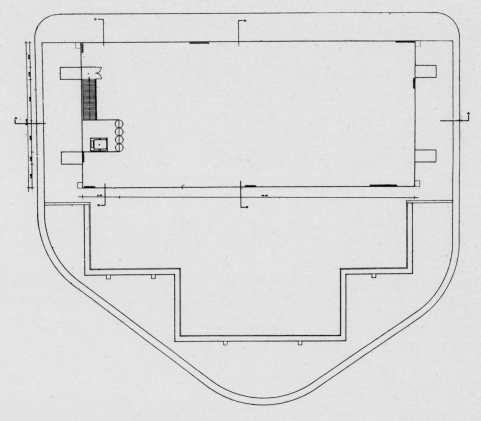

São Paulo Museum of Art: Museum level, in the upper block (code +14.50)

Level of offices, library, temporary exhibitions, and other services in the upper block (code +8.50).

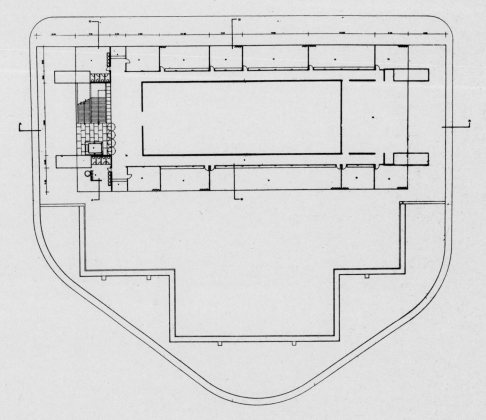

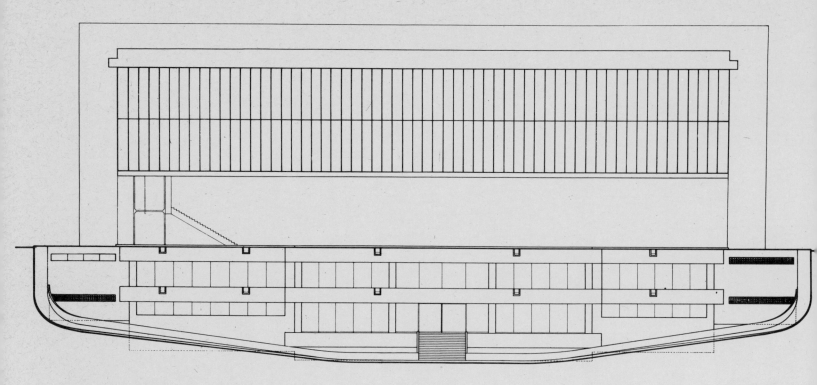

São Paulo Museum of Art: facade as seen from Avenida Nove de Julho. Above, the Belvedere Plaza at the Avenida Paulista level bounded by Obávio Mendes and Plínio Figueiredo Streets.

View of the Museum from the Avenida Paulista side.

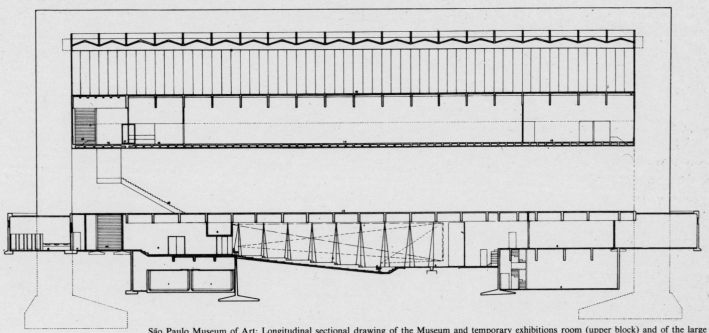

São Paulo Museum of Art: Longitudinal sectional drawing of the Museum and temporary exhibitions room (upper block) and of the large auditorium (basement level).

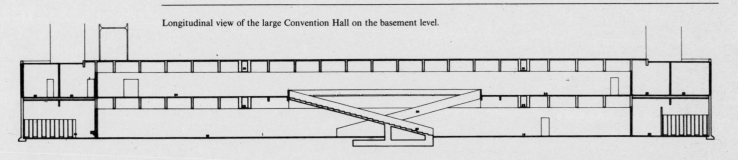

Longitudinal view of the large Convention Hall on the basement level.

Cross sectional view of the Museum, offices, temporary exhibitions hall (upper block) and the large basement room separated by the open-air Belvedere.

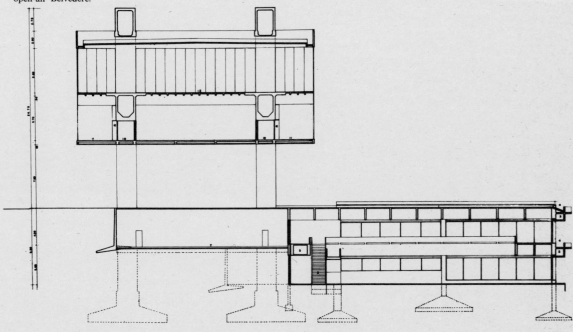

SELECTED BIBLIOGRAPHY

BARDI, P. M.: *Art Treasures of the São Paulo Museum and the Development of Art in Brazil.* Harry N. Abrams, New York, 1956.

BARDI, P. M. and ADHÉMAR, HÉLÈNE: *L'Art Français au Musée d'Art de São Paulo,* "Art et Style", Paris, 1954. English edition, Soho Gallery, London, 1954.

BARDI, P. M.: *The Arts in Brazil—A New Museum at São Paulo.* Edizone del Milione, Milan, 1956.

BARDI, P. M.: *Profile of the New Brazilian Art.* Phaidon Press, London, 1970.

CHATEAUBRIAND, ASSIS and BARDI, P. M., ed.: *Catalogo das pinturas, escultares e tapeçarias do Museu de Arte.* São Paulo, 1963.

MUSÉE DE L'ORANGERIE: *Chefs-d'Oeuvre du Musée d'Art de São Paulo.* Editions des Musées Nationaux, Paris, 1953.

THE ARTS COUNCIL OF GREAT BRITAIN: *Masterpieces from the São Paulo Museum of Art at the Tate Gallery.* London, 1954.

THE METROPOLITAN MUSEUM OF ART: *Masterpieces from the São Paulo Museum of Art.* New York, 1957.

THE TOLEDO MUSEUM OF ART: *One Hundred Paintings from the São Paulo Museum of Art.* Toledo, 1957.

INDEX OF ILLUSTRATIONS

169

INDEX OF NAMES

Note: Italic numbers refer to names mentioned in captions.

GENERAL INDEX